*In heartfelt gratitude to my fellow Marists
on the general leadership team in Rome:
Joaquin Fernandez, Peter Westerman,
Larry Duffy, John Harhager, Günther Koller;
to my sisters and brothers in the Marist congregations,
and to all who seek the growth of a church
with a Marian face*

Fritz Arnold SM

Like Mary

TOWARDS CHRISTIAN MATURITY
IN THE TWENTY-FIRST CENTURY

Translated from the German by
Denis Green SM

the columba press

First published in 2001 by
the columba press
55A Spruce Avenue, Stillorgan Industrial Park,
Blackrock, Co Dublin

Cover by Bill Bolger
Origination by The Columba Press
Printed in Ireland by ColourBooks Ltd, Dublin

ISBN 1 85607 321 1

Contents

Foreword

The experience of radical change in the western world today extends to every facet of life, reaching into the values by which we live, and not least into the domain of religious faith. To judge by declining church attendance and widespread reluctance to accept church rulings, many are finding it difficult to be active members, not to speak of their encouraging others to become Christians.

In spite of doubt and the blatant materialism of much of our culture, many people invest a great deal of themselves in helping others, and some actively look for spirituality and a deeper meaning to their lives. These were the kind of people who would formerly have been active Christians, yet their impression of 'church' is such that nowadays they often do not think of looking there for inspiration and spiritual experience.

I have written this book because I want to contribute to my readers' discovery of Christ in their own lives and in the life of the church, so that in today's conditions they can grow to full stature personally and within the faith community. I recall the almost prophetic word of Karl Rahner that Christians of the future would only be able to live their faith with conviction, if they were in some way mystics.

Personally, I do not see the modern world in a basically negative light, nor do I believe what is happening to the church necessarily indicates a decline. Of course there are usually some negative aspects where human beings are concerned, and that is certainly the case at present. Yet fundamentally I believe the human race is undergoing a profound change in the very way it thinks and approaches life, and I see this as a positive development, in line with God's creation of humankind. I believe too that the church is on the rough passage from being a highly visible, structured institution to being more evidently an instrument of God's mercy and a vehicle of the Spirit. I see this development portrayed in Mary, the mother of Jesus.

Of course I am fully aware Mary is a stumbling block for some Christians. For younger Catholics in the western world, she often means little. For many Christians of Protestant tradition, Catholic mariology is repugnant because they see it as intruding on the central place of Christ, and giving rise to an unbalanced theology. I too share these sensitivities. Exaggerated forms of marian devotion do, in fact, tend to produce a lopsided expression of faith.

I am concerned to concentrate on the core of the faith. I believe misgivings will be dispelled if we see Mary as she has been portrayed in the scriptures. With her whole being, Mary refers to Jesus as the centre of her life: 'Do whatever he tells you' (Jn 2:5). If we accept her, the servant of the Lord, as a portrait of our own spiritual life, she will straight away refer us, as individuals and as faith community, to her own unobtrusive position, so that we place Christ the Saviour at the centre, and not ourselves.

I am also sensitive that some readers, who come across New Age religious beliefs and practices, may wonder if I give too large a place to personal spiritual experience, or to the evolution of a new consciousness and a new humanity.

In my presentation I have addressed some questions that are dealt with in quite different contexts from mine. For me it is important to throw light on these matters from a Christian standpoint, where the spiritual maturity of the individual and the faith community can only be achieved through the grace of God.

The spirituality of my own congregation, the Marists, has been a valuable incentive to me, but also the thinking of the Christian mystics of the Middle Ages and later, writers such as Tauler, Angelus Silesius and many others.

The English language edition

I know that today, many people are intensely interested in religious topics, but like visitors to a strange country, they may have difficulty with unfamiliar words and names. I would like this book to be helpful to as many as possible, so in the English language edition an asterisk * follows such words and names the first time they occur; an explanatory note is to found on page 156. The full reference apparatus in the German edition has been shortened.

I want to thank my friend and fellow Marist, Fr Denis Green, for his sensitive translation, which is more than a mere translation, and has in many respects improved the original.

May this work contribute to the discovery of Christ in our own lives and in the life of the church. May we so bear ourselves that he may grow to full stature in us and in the community of believers. May our actions serve life, growth and the unfolding of life, so that many more people may come to the fullness of life.

Fritz Arnold SM
Rome, 1 January 2000
Solemnity of Mary, Mother of God

Introduction

Growth and change

Life has to do with growth and change. Becoming, maturing and bearing fruit are stages in every earthly life. Conception, birth, growth, fruitfulness, suffering, death and new life sprouting up again are phases of it. These are also evident in specific ways in the growth of each person's spiritual life, in the spiritual growth of the faith community and indeed of the whole human community. Thus, with sensitive insight, the church arranged to hold its festive celebrations to correspond with the seasons of the then known world, the northern hemisphere. Christmas comes after the shortest day in the year when daylight is lengthening once more; Easter falls as spring arrives and new life burgeons and blooms; Pentecost is celebrated as the fruits of the earth begin to ripen. The annual cycle is a profound symbol of growth.

Today, more and more people express their conviction that we and the whole of humanity have now to go through a massive process of change, and to advance to an entirely new consciousness. As church we share in the joys, hopes, anxieties and problems of our contemporaries, and we share their concern as we also undergo radical change. As a community of believers, we too must pass through dark places, seek and struggle as we look for directions on the way.

Mary

When we bring attentive faith to the deepest promises of the Christian message -- that we are temples of the Holy Spirit, that Christ himself will be born in us and grow to full stature in us -- we can learn still more from Mary. She is the woman who actually brought Jesus Christ into the world two thousand years ago, and cared for him as he grew to maturity. The most profound mystical truths concerning the birth of God in the human race, entry into the mystery of the life and death of Jesus Christ, new life in the Spirit, are all perfectly portrayed in Mary. She stands at the point where divine life breaks into the world. Receptive to God, she is at the source of life, fruitful for others.

Mary is the image of the human race redeemed. In her, God shows us a picture of what he has done for us, and of what he will do.

Gregory Nazianzen* says that as Mary bore Christ in her womb and then brought him into the world, so should the human soul bear Christ as though in his mother's womb, and bring him into the world through living a spiritual life. So, too, Angelus Silesius*: 'You should become Mary and bear the son of God within you.'

Mary is a type*, a personification or embodiment of the church. In her there appears a renewed picture of the church, a church where the accent is on service rather than on hierarchy and on law.

Overview

In the first section, we examine how the Bible presents Mary as the image of faith. Though relatively little is said about her, we do get quite a good picture because the few places where she is referred to have all to do with crucial moments in her life as mother of Jesus. In this section we shall also look at the stages in Mary's spiritual way.

In a second section, I want to illustrate how these stages recur in our own spiritual development. We too must conceive Christ, bring him into the world, allow him to grow within us, and, passing through phases of change and suffering, come to a new mission. We shall specially look at how God is born in the soul.

In a third section, I will speak of the mystery of the church. We shall see how the church lives because she continually conceives the Spirit within her, and in missionary stance, proclaims this Spirit to the world. The church too must go through radical change, and pass through dark places *en route* to new life. We shall see how the marian face of the church is gradually emerging in our day.

CHAPTER ONE

Mary, embodiment of Faith

Before we reflect on Mary, Mother of our Lord Jesus Christ, it is really important to clarify her place in salvation history. At the core of the Bible and of all Christian statements stands the person and message of Jesus Christ, and their place in our lives. Mary is only concerned in so far as she serves the coming of Jesus and points to Christ. Consequently, the Bible speaks of her only a few times, and we must take care in our reflections not to reverse this unobtrusive quality of Mary

In the course of history marian devotions got out of hand. All kinds of fanciful notions were aired, pious fantasies making up for the absence of information. We are certainly not going to try here to reconstruct a kind of 'Life of Mary' from the biblical data, nor to produce an imaginative portrait by reading more into the texts than they contain.

Mary will continue to occupy for us the hidden place accorded to her in the Bible, and so she will become for us an image of faith. Theological statements about Mary are correct in so far as they are finally statements about God and about his saving dealings with his people; or statements about people as having been redeemed. Mariology* is not a teaching about the special privileges of Mary. If the Fathers of the Church* talk about Mary, it is because they want to praise God by doing so. Mary is for them a prism through which the divine breaks in upon us. She is for them a mirror in which the revelation of God in Jesus Christ is viewed from another angle and seen in a new light. It is idle to squabble about whether the official statements about Mary are necessary to salvation. Theoretically we could do without a mariology, but in fact we already find in the Bible, and still more in the early tradition of the church, attempts to see the saving work of God mirrored in Mary.

These efforts spring from the human need to express the mystery of God in image and symbol, not in abstract concepts alone. Publications on the subject of Mary appearing since the Second Vatican Council have contributed to the advent of a more balanced mariology

Although Mary is mentioned only in a few places in the bible, these are always at important points in her life. Luke speaks of Mary at the beginning of Jesus' life (annunciation, birth, childhood), and likewise at the beginning of the church (Pentecost). In John's gospel, Mary only appears twice, but again on very outstanding occasions: at the start of Jesus' public activity (the wedding feast at Cana) and at the end (standing by the cross). Such well defined situations have also a symbolic meaning. They show how Mary is present in a hidden way, at special junctures when something new is happening. In the Bible, the proclamation of Jesus Christ, Redeemer of all the world, is published in the form of an historical account. The biblical statements are all written in the light of the Easter experience. The literary genre* must be taken into particular consideration in dealing with the principal source for mariological statements, namely, the accounts of Jesus' childhood.

In order to take in the full import and richness of the biblical accounts we must, as it were, venture into the simplicity of childhood again, and allow the biblical texts to work directly on us, notwithstanding the knowledge we have acquired from critical research. The philosopher, Peter Wust, believes that true wisdom consists in an attitude of simplicity, allowing truth to be accepted like a child. Only thus can we become aware of the drama of God's breaking into the world, contained in the embellished childhood texts. While realising the difficulty of accepting and transmitting this truth, we discover the greater possibilities God is opening up, and we do not interpret the text out of existence by insisting on historical exegesis*.

Contemplating Mary should help us advance considerably

towards the mystical dimension of faith. By 'mystical' is meant the ability to live from the transcendent dimension of faith. A genuine mysticism opens the eyes of faith and the doors of the heart, to become aware of the all present and active God. Such mysticism is far from looking for the extraordinary, for ecstasy, etc. Seeking for the extraordinary even interferes with the unfolding of a genuine, healthy mysticism. So our attention will not be directed to marian apparitions or messages. Rather, we shall bring into relief how, by considering Mary, the deepest truths of faith are disclosed in a personal way.

Of course this mystical dimension is little developed in our present-day faith consciousness. Today there is a widespread deficit of mysticism, both in theology and in faith life. We shall only be able to meet the challenge of our time creatively and productively if we advance to the mystical dimension of faith. In the nineteen-sixties Karl Rahner* pioneered the way: 'The true believer of tomorrow will either be a mystic, one who experiences God, or he will not exist at all.'[1] The contemplation of Mary will help us to understand better the mystical dimension of faith, and above all allow it to enter into our own lives.

Marian devotion and mariology have always indicated with seismographic exactness, highs and lows in the faith condition of Christians. Thus at the time when theology predominantly emphasised the divinity of Christ and neglected his humanity, the devotion of the people to Mary occupied the place which really belonged to the humanity. To the extent that pneumatology* was neglected, Mary took the place of the Holy Spirit.

At a time when it was important to maintain the place a person held in the pre-established social order, Mary was principally seen as the lowly handmaid of the Lord. In our time, in so far as there is a greater awareness of injustice in the world and there is a struggle for justice, Mary becomes a champion of that struggle. In Leonardo Boff's liberation theology, the Magnificat becomes a great Prayer of Freedom in which Mary praises God, who puts down the mighty from their thrones and exalts the lowly. As feminist theology opposes the disadvantaging of women in society, Mary again serves as an identifying symbol.

The contemplation of Mary appears as a valuable help to make up for the mystical deficit of our time. The name Miriam, which crops up in various places in the Old Testament and was given to Mary at birth, already points the way. The Hebrew word *miriam* means, approximately, to be born, stand upright, come to full life. The word Mary has therefore something to do with growth, unfolding and fullness of life.

As Mary conceived and bore Christ, so will Christ also be conceived and born in each one of us. He wills to be conceived and born in the community of believers as well. When we look at Mary, the deep truths of faith open to us in a personalised way.

1. RESPONSIVE TO GOD

With the Bible to hand, if we want to picture Mary, the Mother of Jesus, the New Testament stories are an all important source. While the earliest evangelist, Mark, begins at once with the activity of Jesus, Matthew and Luke enquire about his childhood. The gospel writers are not concerned to produce an historical narrative, but to present a declaration of faith. Matthew wants to proclaim Jesus as Liberator, one whose coming into the world was fraught with as much danger as that of Moses'. Luke will present the childhood as a link between the Old and New Covenants, beginning with Jesus.

The Bible has a predilection for beginnings. It likes telling beginning stories – beginnings in faith. Much is concealed in a beginning: path, dynamic, direction, programme. The beginning of Jesus' life, his coming into the world, is already bound up with Mary, his mother. Her 'Yes' made the incarnation possible. That is the subject of the annunciation scene.

This scene can be described as a real dialogue between God and humanity, in which the partners respond to each other. God takes the initiative, resolves upon the work of redemption and finds in Mary a partner ready to hear. He chooses her out and speaks to her: 'Hail full of grace, the Lord is with you!'(Lk 1:28). In you, Mary, I have chosen the woman who pleases my heart, a willing instrument, ready for service. God finds in Mary a human being who allows herself to enter and dialogue with him. She is filled with the Holy Spirit. The reality of God breaks directly into her life. It is a truth which cannot be played down, and which challenges her totally.

In later times, theological reflection maintained that God's grace and his choice of Mary accompanied her from her conception and birth. There was a growing awareness that in Mary, God had prepared a worthy dwelling for his coming and that he had, on that account, preserved her from original sin. As before sunrise the sky reddens and proclaims the coming day, so in Mary dawned the light of the redemption. A corresponding feast emerged in Constantinople in the ninth century, was then celebrated in southern Italy, and from the fifteenth century in England. On 8 December 1854 Pope Pius IX finally declared the teaching on the Immaculate Conception a binding article of faith.

In the annunciation scene Mary becomes aware that she is specially chosen by God, and God makes known to her that he has sought her out to be the dwelling place for his coming into the world.

Fright

Mary's first reaction to the tremendous promise made by God was understandably one of fright. She was left speechless. But she did not run away. She did not block out dialogue. She reflected rather on what this greeting might mean. Silently Mary held fast to the surprising word and took it in. This points to openness, trust, readiness. So God's word can reach its end and have its effect in her life. God reveals himself more intimately. 'You will conceive in your womb and bear a son, and you shall call his name Jesus' (Lk 1:31). Mary now feels appalled as she is faced with something contrary to all human understanding. She is to become a mother while remaining a virgin. God's plans for her life are infinitely greater and better than her own plans.

Something of her feelings shows in every conversation God

has with a human being. God wants to break into the life of each one of us and to lead us out of the narrowness of our human limitations.

Questioning

Mary makes enquiries. Her first words are not ones of unquestioning acceptance. She does not give a swift agreement to something she could not fulfil, but first enquires. In that way the Word of God can register in all the fibres of her life, not only in the area of emotions, but also in her mind. Mary questions from her point of view, but does not make an absolute of this viewpoint. God wants seeking, wrestling people. He accepts that we are never finished with him. True purification can only take place if we allow God to penetrate into every area of our life. If we really wrestle with God, he will give us an answer with which he breaks through the narrowness of our human capacities. God points to the greater possibilities at his disposal. 'The Holy Spirit will come upon you, and the power of the Most High will overshadow you' (Lk 1:35.) 'For with God nothing will be impossible' (Lk 1:37). God can show us possibilities, where we ourselves could see no more.

Readiness

Trusting in these greater capacities of God, Mary then gives her agreement in faith. 'I am the handmaid of the Lord; let it be to me according to your word' (Lk 1:38). She utters a fully personal 'Yes' of faith, that embraces the whole realm of human feeling, thinking and willing. She holds to this agreement her whole life long. God's Word can thus take root in her breast and she can finally bring Jesus into the world. In a very hidden way, the divine promises begin to be fulfilled. She conceives by the Holy Spirit, becomes pregnant.

2. EXPECTATION AND ENCOUNTER

Alone with a great secret

When the angel leaves Mary she is filled with the power of God and with its promise. The divine life begins to germinate in her. The God-human begins to grow as an embryo in her womb. But this wonderful pregnancy is fraught with a great problem for her. She cannot speak to anyone about the overwhelming experience of her life. How should she tell Joseph, to whom she is engaged, what has happened to her? How will he react when he notices she has become pregnant? Anxiety arises in her that he could dismiss her. Then she would be doomed to death. Carlo Caretto, in his book on Mary, tells about a cruel experience in the desert. A woman was stoned by her fellow tribes folk, because she was unfaithful before marriage and got pregnant. This experience enabled him to grasp what Mary had to go through after the annunciation. 'On that evening I felt for the first time that I had drawn close to the mystery of Mary. For the first time I felt she was no motionless, wax statue on an altar, got up as a queen, but saw her as a sister, saw her close to me, sitting on the sand of this world, with worn-out sandals, like mine, her limbs just as weary. I felt Mary was crouching in the sand, close beside me, a little weak, helpless in her wondrous but unmistakable pregnancy'.[2] After the divine encounter she is alone with a great mystery, a secret she cannot share with anyone, because no one would understand. A great solitude begins to envelop her.

According to Matthew's account, God himself intervenes and overcomes her aloneness. He imparts the mystery of her life to Joseph in a dream, so that the difficult problem for him and Mary is resolved (cf. Mt 1:18-25).

In the divine promise there was talk of Elizabeth also bearing a child, a mystery in her womb. So Mary makes her way to Elizabeth in the hope of being able to speak with her. Before she can give any indication of what has happened to her, Elizabeth senses the divine mystery in Mary and speaks out, filled with the Holy Spirit (cf. Lk 1:42).

An understanding encounter
The meeting of Mary and Elizabeth (Lk 1:39-56), presents a heartfelt, person to person dialogue springing from their en-

counter with God, rendered possible by the hidden presence of Christ in their midst. Each of them senses something of the mystery which the other is bearing within herself. As Mary greets her, Elizabeth is filled with the Holy Spirit. She senses what great things God has done in Mary: 'And blessed is she who believed that there would be a fulfilment of what was spoken to her by the Lord' (Lk 1:45).

It is important to find someone who has understanding for the deepest mystery of the other, to find people with whom we can speak about the divine dimension in the reality of our own life. Spiritual accompaniment, one to one dialogue, are an important mutual spiritual service to allow the divine enter into one's life. A feeling for the divine in one's own life enables us also to develop a feeling for it in other people's.

Because of the heartfelt experience of deeper understanding, Mary is moved to that great act of praise and thanksgiving which is the Magnificat, built around a reminiscence of the Song of Hanna (1 Sam 2:1-10). She expresses her jubilation over the great things God has done. Now she can joyfully accept what God has called her to.

For every woman, expecting a child is a special event. Her life acquires a new and deeper meaning. She feels thanksgiving and joy at the new life growing in her. That is so in a special way for Mary, who now praises God for her wonderful, divinely initiated pregnancy. 'My soul magnifies the Lord, and my spirit rejoices in God my Saviour, for he has regarded the lowly estate of his handmaiden' (Lk 1:46ff). Here a person is praying who has known the greatness of God. To outline her personal experience Mary draws from the treasury of Israel's thousands of years of devotional tradition. She realises she has been enormously enriched by God, and chosen by him. She recognises with a simple, full thanksgiving, and without any pride: 'Behold, henceforth all generations will call me blessed' (Lk 1:48).

Mary knows that in her pregnancy the expectations of generations of humankind are coming to fulfilment. She praises God, not only for the great things he has done in her, but for his mercy, which lasts from generation to generation. She praises God that he has chosen the lowly, in order to perform great things. God is able to reverse existing relationships. It pleases him to make the small great and the great small: 'He has put down the mighty from their thrones, and exalted those of high degree; he has filled the hungry with good things, and the rich he has sent away empty' (Lk 1:52ff). God wants a new world of justice, love and peace. Mary is ready, in joy and humility, to take that place in the history of salvation which God has designed for her.

Now she will live in joyful expectation of the birth of the Saviour, Jesus Christ, whom she is bearing in her womb.

3. INCARNATION

This greatest of events in human history, the incarnation of the Son of God in Jesus Christ, does not take place in a spectacular way, as one could have expected, but in obscurity, poverty and exile. Luke tells how Joseph gets underway with his pregnant wife, making for Bethlehem, the city of David, to be registered in the tax lists, in accordance with the decree of Caesar Augustus. The evangelist stresses that they could not find any lodging. Their searching in vain for shelter is part of many a nativity play. People have no room for Joseph, Mary and the child she is bearing in her womb. They have to spend the night in a stable. And there, away from home, Mary brings her child into the world, a boy. She 'wrapped him in swaddling cloths, and laid him in a manger' (Lk 2:7).

John's gospel describes the same event with the words: 'He came into his own home, but his own people received him not' (Jn 1:11). Homelessness will accompany Jesus from crib to cross.

Ignatius of Loyola* invites us, in the *Spiritual Exercises*, to imagine the circumstances of Jesus birth. We are to picture the cramped unhomeliness of the cave and feel the cold of the night on which Jesus was born. So then shall we reflect how the way of Jesus began in the greatest poverty and ended in abuse and insults at the cross.[3] God lowers himself and becomes one of us, becomes as the least of humans.

We need to be very clear-sighted to be aware of the hidden divinity in the midst of such misery. All too lightly do we pass over his divinity, because we do not care to see the interior greatness within his lowliness. God became a human, so that we may obtain a share in the divine.

Jesus was born at a time when Israel belonged to the Roman Empire and was being exploited by the occupying power; a time when the Pharisees had withdrawn into the ivory tower of strict legalistic piety. Zealots were trying to stir up a movement of political opposition to the Romans, while people out at Qumran had withdrawn into isolation and retreat, impelled by a vision of the final end of all things.

This unsettled time was the living context for the coming of Jesus into our world. Legally, he is the carpenter's son. Very few perceive his divine origins: shepherds in the fields, old Simeon, the widow Anna in the Temple. Others, like Herod, feel anxiety and react with blind rage. So Jesus, Mary and Joseph must take flight. The fate of Jesus, from the start, lies under threat. But the embrace of God's fidelity is also with them: Mary and Joseph, as Matthew relates, are warned in a dream to flee to Egypt, to save their son's life and their own (cf. Mt 2:13f). They become refugees. Matthew, writing for Jewish Christians, intentionally points to Egypt, the place where the people of Israel had to spend long years as prisoners. According to Matthew, Jesus also shared the fate of his people abroad for a number of years .[4] In striking resemblance to the story of Moses, Jesus is under threat from the start, according to Matthew, but he too is protected by the loving direction of God.

Thus the greatest event in human history takes place, according to God's will, in obscurity, poverty and isolation. One needs a capacity to see into the hidden in order to become aware of God in these inconspicuous situations. May God grant us his eyes to see what is truly great, what is the treasure and the precious pearl of our lives.

4. GROWTH AND FRUITFULNESS

Mary is the witness to how the divine mystery grew in Jesus during his childhood and youth. Beside her, Jesus grew in age and wisdom before God and people (Lk 2:52). Mary is very attentive to this divine mystery. In the childhood story, Luke twice emphasises how Mary kept in her heart and considered everything she had experienced (cf. Lk 2:19; Lk 2:52). In her, God's word fell on fruitful ground. Mary always learned something new about her child, because the fullness of his being was never expressible all at once, in its entirety. The riches hidden in revelation can never be imparted, except in single pieces. Mary is the image of all who receive the Word in the right way, image of believers, image of the church.

The hidden years in Nazareth

The gospel only reports in one verse the long years of Jesus' and Mary's hidden life in Nazareth.[5] 'He went down with them and came to Nazareth, and was obedient to them' (Lk 2:51). Astonishingly, received theology hardly concerned itself with this verse, which refers to thirty years of Jesus' life.[6] For St Bernard* the divine paradox is revealed: the Son of God, humbly, obediently submitting himself to people. Ignatius of Loyola*, in his *Spiritual Exercises*, invites the retreatant to reflect on the life of our Lord Jesus Christ between his twelfth and thirtieth year.[7] Of course the text is exceedingly brief, but since that time all who have made the *Spiritual Exercises* have been linked with the mystery of Nazareth. It was not really until the seventeenth century that theological writers took up the mystery of Jesus in Nazareth as a main theme. For Boudon* the entire life of Jesus is hidden, beginning in Nazareth and ending on the cross. For Charles de Foucauld* and his companions to understand as perfectly as possible the life of Jesus at Nazareth will be an aim worth striving after.

The Marian interpretation of Luke's verse 2:51 is still more sparse than the christological.* For Venerable Bede* this text points to the nature of the contemplative life. As Mary guarded and venerated the divine mystery of Jesus in Nazareth over thirty years, so should the contemplative Christian worship prayerfully and remain hidden, like Mary. Only in the eighteenth century with authors such as Rouville and Grou* did meditation on the hidden life of Mary come to the fore.

The situation is not very different for veneration of the Holy Family, which only began to flourish in the nineteenth century. Luke's verse 2.51 gives the impression that Jesus grew up in ordered, peaceful conditions. Of course he does not remain silent about pressures and misunderstandings during that time. When Jesus, now twelve years old, remained behind in the Temple, Mary and Joseph go looking for him everywhere. When they find him in the Temple, they say: 'Son, why have you treated us so? Behold, your Father and I have been looking for you anxiously?' (Lk 2:48). An understandable reproof, but it also expresses that Jesus grew up so normally in Nazareth that Mary and Joseph paid hardly any particular heed to his divinity. They have to learn again that God is his Father, that his real home is his Father's house, the Temple.

Whoever draws close to Jesus will not be spared from misunderstanding. Mary, too, is not immune from misunderstanding, but she is ready for her faith to grow. She preserves all these things in her heart (Lk 2:51). As mother of Jesus, she remains intimately bound to the fate of her son in every life situation, in joy and in pain. It is prophesied to her by old Simeon: 'A sword shall pierce through your own soul also' (Lk 2:35). This word points already to the conflicts which Jesus will meet in his public ministry. The contradiction he meets with will also happen to Mary. A person who relies on Jesus must be ready to go on the way with him, right to the cross. The 'yes' of faith spoken by her at the annunciation had to extend beyond that moment and become a reality over her whole life

The public ministry of Jesus
During the public ministry of Jesus, Mary steps into the background. The disciples are now close to Jesus, those whom he

called to follow him and whom he initiated into the mystery of his being and mission. At the centre of his activity stand the men to whom he proclaimed the message of the kingdom of God, promised healing and salvation, pardoned and promised new life.

The relatives of Jesus do not understand

In the earliest gospel the mother of Jesus is spoken about in only one place, and one could almost describe this as an anti-marian text. For it says here that the relatives of Jesus, among them Mary, were having difficulty in understanding him. They considered his behaviour was crazy and wanted to take him back home (Mk 3:21). While Jesus is preaching, his mother and brothers are waiting outside and enquiring for him. He is told: 'Your mother and your brethren are outside, asking for you' (Mk 3:32). Looking at the circle of people sitting around him, Jesus answers: 'Here are my mother and my brethren! Whoever does the will of God is my brother and sister, and mother'(Mk 3:34). This declaration puts Mary in the group of outsiders. The real family of believers are his disciples – they are the insiders.

Matthew corrects in a positive sense the impression Mark gives of Mary and the natural family of Jesus, and Luke finally leaves out altogether the contrast between the unbelieving family of Jesus and the true family of believers. He simply says: 'My mother and my brethren are those who hear the word of God and do it' (Lk 8:21).

The priority of spiritual over family relationship is stated in Luke 11:27. We hear how a woman in the crowd calls out: 'Blessed is the womb that bore you, and the breast that you sucked.' And we hear Jesus answer: 'Blessed rather are those who hear the word of God and keep it.'

For Luke, Mary is both: she is the mother who brought Jesus into the world, and she is the one who heard the word of God and followed it. She is not only mother of Jesus on the physical level, but also on the spiritual plane.

The first sermon of Jesus in Nazareth

Of course this fidelity to the word of God cost Mary a great deal in a family and a village that disapproved of Jesus during the greater part of his public ministry. According to Luke Jesus gave his first sermon in his home town. He reports how Jesus was initially accepted with enthusiasm, but was then rejected, driven out of the town. and hustled to the brow of a hill to be thrown down (cf. Lk 4:29).

It must have been difficult for Mary to live in such an environment, but she kept all the words of the Lord and pondered them in her heart. She was always alert for God's word and the needs of his people.

Cana: The first miracle of Jesus

Just how alert Mary was to the needs of people is very strikingly evident in the scene with which the evangelist John begins the public ministry of Jesus.[8] At a wedding feast in Cana, Mary becomes aware there is no more wine left. She calls her son's attention to the crisis. Although Jesus' reaction does not seem encouraging, she says to the servers: 'Do whatever he tells you' (Jn 2:5). With her whole being she points to Jesus and away from herself. She trusts in his help. Mary's faith precedes this first revelation of divine power. As her faith preceded and accompanied the coming of Jesus on earth, so now her powerful faith is here at the beginning of his public activity. Through it, she arouses others to place their trust in him. Her life is a living invitation to believe in Jesus Christ. Mary prepares the ground at the marriage feast, so that Jesus performs his first miracle there, and begins his public ministry.

What Jesus says to the servers is significant too: 'Fill the jars with water' (Jn 2:7). He is inviting them to do what lies within their human capacity, as though to say: 'You do what you can do, even if it is only drawing water. Fill up the jar of your life and I will turn it into choice wine; but leave it empty, and there will be nothing there for me to change.' The servers do as the Lord says, and Jesus begins his ministry, changing the water into wine.

While Jesus is proclaiming the message of the kingdom of God, healing the sick and granting pardon, Mary steps back. Then, when most people and even his disciples draw away from him, we discover her there again: she is one of the very few standing by the cross.

5. THE PASSION: MARY BESIDE THE CROSS

Jesus' whole life is pervaded by passion experiences: the disciples' lack of understanding; rejection by the Pharisees. His most loving attention is in vain; his total self-giving finds no response; his best intentions are misconstrued. All that must have weighed upon him, discouraging and crippling his will to love. An inner passion precedes the history of exterior suffering.

Likewise, Mary's suffering does not begin with Jesus being condemned to death. Tradition has had a feeling for this, and names several 'Sorrows of Mary', such as those expressed in the commemoration of the 'Seven Dolours': the announcement by Simeon of suffering to come; the flight into Egypt; Jesus' staying behind in the Temple as a boy; the sorrow and suffering of Mary as Jesus made his way to the cross; finally, her presence there at the crucifixion, the taking down of his body from the cross and its being laid in the tomb.

The sufferings of Jesus, and also those of Mary, are outward, physical, but still more are they inward and spiritual. They are indeed inflicted by antagonists, but still more by his own disciples, denying and betraying their Master, their Lord. One of his own betrays him for thirty silver coins. While he suffers in agony, the disciples fall asleep. When he is taken prisoner they save their skins. By the cross we do not see Peter, the head of the group, nor the other disciples.

Mary, a few other women and 'the disciple whom Jesus loved' are the notable exceptions. These witness to their discipleship right to the end. They stand by the cross and share the experience of Jesus, abandoned and God-forsaken. They hear his desolate cry: 'My God, my God, why have you forsaken me?' (Mt 27:46). In that hour Mary may have remembered how she was

called at the annunciation: 'You will conceive in your womb and
bear a son ... He will be great, and will be called Son of the Most
High, and the Lord God will give to him the throne of his father
David, and he will reign over the house of Jacob for ever, and of
his kingdom there will be no end' (Lk 1:32f).

Mary may have asked herself: what has become of that call?
Instead of the promised throne, her son is now hanging there on
a shameful gibbet. Instead of any sort of sovereignty, only total
helplessness is there. What has become of the promise? Why is
God allowing this? Why does he not put to shame those scoffers
and their jeering, 'Come down from the cross'? This must have
been the darkest hour of Mary's life, having to stand helplessly
by while her only son must undergo such cruel suffering.

In the midst of this deepest darkness, Jesus turned to his
mother, Mary, and glancing towards the disciple he loved, he
said: 'Woman, behold your son!' and turning to the disciple he
said: 'Behold your mother!' (Jn 19:26f).

Instead of being mother of Jesus, Mary now receives a new
maternity: she must surrender her son at the cross, and in his
place the disciple whom Jesus loved is given into her care. That
privileged disciple, significantly never named, does not refer
just to an historical person. He sheds light on what it means to be
a Christian, and in him we Christians see what the aim of our
Christian life is to be. As readers of the gospel, we are invited to
find ourselves in the disciple whom Jesus loved. If we do so, we
will also understand that Mary is our mother, the mother of believers, the mother and image of the church.[9]

Meanwhile this hopeful word from the mouth of Jesus is
spoken into the darkness. The evangelists say a great darkness
broke over the land from the sixth to the ninth hour. In the suffering and dying of Jesus the whole world experienced darkness,
the eclipse of God.

Mary and the beloved disciple of Jesus experienced together
in darkness this death of Jesus. According to the witness of the
oldest gospel: 'Jesus uttered a loud cry, and breathed his last'
(Mk 15:37). John's gospel testifies that a soldier opened the side

of Jesus and that blood and water flowed from it (cf. Jn 19:34). Medical science has concluded that Jesus did not die the usual death of the crucified. Normally a crucified man died when all his physical powers of resistance were exhausted and he suffocated. Jesus must have died because his heart was physically broken, torn by psychic pain, inflicted – we may add – by all our sins. In any case, Mary and the disciple sensed the love of Jesus, how the heart of Jesus was now open to all men and women.

At this moment Mary becomes the one who is full of grief, the 'Pietà', holding her dead son to her bosom. What must she have felt? Mary bore Jesus in her womb when she was pregnant and visited Elisabeth. She bore him at her breast when he was a little child and the wise men came from the East. During his public ministry he had proclaimed that we are all hidden in God's bosom. And now, after her son's cruel death, she is holding him again against her bosom. This is for her the hour of deepest disillusionment and darkness.

The church recommends us on Holy Saturday to meditate on the situation after the death of Jesus, on the seeming absence of God, the darkness of God, the silence of God, the death of God. Mary and the followers of Jesus lived through that situation in all its brutality. The death of Jesus was the collapse of all the hopes they had vested in him. The disciples on the road to Emmaus express that: 'We hoped that he was the one to redeem Israel' (Lk 1:32). And now all these horrors had happened.

The annunciation had surely aroused great expectations in Mary also. 'He will be great and will be called Son of the Most High' (Lk 1:32). What had become of that? Have I chased after an hallucination? With what enthusiasm I sang the Magnificat: 'The Almighty works marvels for me, holy his name … henceforth all ages will call me blessed!' (Lk 147f). Why has God proved so powerless in this situation? Why has he allowed the best man earth has ever known to die so brutally.

A dark tangle of despondency built up in Mary. In the gospels we hear nothing of her darkness, but rather of the disciples'. Says Peter: 'I am going out fishing', and the others say:

'We'll come too' (Jn 21:3). That is as though to say: 'Let us go back to our old job. Being together with Jesus was a wonderful time, but unfortunately it all went wrong. For Thomas this gloom simply did not lift even when the others reported enthusiastically to him their experience of the resurrection. Mary of Magdala wants to anoint the body of Jesus. When she finds the tomb empty it is not a cause of joy for her, but of deeper sorrow, because now someone has stolen the body. Only when she hears her name does she recognise the Risen One in the figure she had supposed was the gardener.

Mary, the Mother of Jesus, no doubt experienced great darkness after the death of Jesus, but she endured it with faith. Doubtless that is why Saturday has been especially consecrated to her. After the disaster, humiliation and pain of Good Friday, only Mary remained true through the emptiness of Holy Saturday. So can we imagine how she experienced all the more deeply the joy of Easter.

6. A NEW MISSION: MARY AND THE RISEN JESUS

In the Bible we find wonderful accounts of meetings between the Risen Jesus and people with whom he had already had in-depth encounter during his life. The gospel of Luke describes the meeting of disciples with the Risen One on the road to Emmaus (cf. Lk 24:13-35), John's gospel the moving meetings between the Risen Jesus and Mary of Magdala, Thomas, Peter and the disciple whom he loved (cf. Jn 20, 25). But there is nowhere described any meeting between Mary and the Risen Jesus. As during the public ministry, so now, she steps back.

Nevertheless, in the history of piety there are efforts to imagine such a meeting. Thus, for example, Ignatius of Loyola invites us in his *Spiritual Exercises* to make a meditation on it. We are invited to empathise with Mary in her interior communion with Jesus, which suggests such a meeting.[10] But how would that be possible in the absence of any biblical statement about it?

It seems to me we can best do this by taking up once more what is said about the disciple whom Jesus loved and applying it to Mary. Like the disciple, she was certainly sensitive in the highest degree to the hidden presence of the Lord. Just as this disciple 'saw and believed' (Jn 20:8), so in faith she was able to see what lay behind visible things. Just as the Beloved Disciple was far more spiritually alert than the other disciples, and thus arrived more swiftly at the tomb, so also is Mary more spiritually open.

In the disciple whom Jesus loved, we can also best sense what took place in the meeting of Mary with the Risen Jesus. She was, more than anyone else, open and receptive to the Lord, had shown him her love and received the Lord's love. She followed him to the cross. And so she, more than any other, will have known the presence of the Risen One. We might very well imagine the word: 'It is the Lord' (Jn 21:7), as a word spoken by her.

While all the others, in their encounter with the risen Lord, were called to a change in their lives, Mary and the disciple whom Jesus loved, were to remain as they were. Peter, who wanted to do everything himself, must learn to let go of the rudder and surrender the steering of his life to the Lord. Thomas, with his reason, wants to form his own picture of reality, and he has to learn to believe others and to trust the Lord. Mary of Magdala, who wants to hold onto the Lord for herself, must learn to share his presence with others. The Beloved Disciple, and certainly Mary as well, are, on the other hand, to remain as they are. She who had conceived by the Holy Spirit will, after the ascension of the Lord, teach the disciples how to wait in the right way for the Holy Spirit.

Mary among the apostles
There is only one place in the Bible – and that is a very short passage – in which Mary is spoken of as praying with the apostles and waiting for the coming of the Holy Spirit (cf. Acts 1:13). Luke, at the beginning of the Acts of the Apostles, refers to the period at the start of the church, and also to Mary. She is there, where there is something decisively new taking place. As she was open to the call of God at the annunciation and conceived

by the Holy Spirit, now she is also with the apostles in the upper room waiting with them for the coming of the Spirit on the young church. Just as in the birth of Jesus she played a central role, now she is to be present with maternal care at the birth of the church (cf. below, chapter 3). Mary throws light on how the spiritual life of the individual and the community of the church is engendered.

Of course the New Testament says nothing about the kind of role Mary fulfilled afterwards in the circle of apostles. It is simply said she was 'there'. Was being there more a contemplative or an active presence? Ambrose* gave rise to the notion that in the apostolic circle Mary had the task of instructing (*magistra apostolorum*). No one else was so close to her son as she, and she brought home to the apostles much about the personal mystery of her son. Bernard of Clairvaux* and Brigit of Sweden* added to the teaching office of Mary thoughts about her having undertaken the position of consoler and counsellor. The great theologian of the Reformation, Melancthon* had no problem with such notions and said Mary led by her counsel.[11] Since the sixteenth and seventeenth centuries an increasingly active role among the apostles in the early church is ascribed to Mary.

An extreme point in this development is reached in the work of Maria d'Agreda*, who devotes no less than twenty-six chapters to the life of Mary among the apostles! She is able to recount how Mary helped them, not only by prayer, but by her active presence in the young church. She counselled the apostles to live irreproachable lives, and helped them to discern spirits when faced with important decisions. She prompted them to celebrate the first eucharist. Peter obtained her advice when sending the apostles out to various parts of the world. No doubt about it, a very active role is ascribed to the Mother of God in the work of Maria d'Agreda! Her presence in the primitive church becomes a model for active apostolic life and work.

Nevertheless, from our viewpoint today, the notion that one can know everything possible about the life of Mary is very strange. With Maria d'Agreda we reach an extreme case of reading things into the Bible.

Quite the contrary, it seems to me important to underline the hidden role of Mary, as it appears in the New Testament account. Mary had a hidden presence among the apostles, because Christ occupied the central position. Yet in spite of her being hidden, she is exceedingly effective.

According as people reflected on the active role of Mary at the beginning of the church, the question also arose about her role at the end of time. On this subject, of course, we find practically nothing in the early church. Only in the heyday of marian piety during the eighteenth and nineteenth centuries do these ideas become significant, as for Grignon de Montfort*, François Cloriviere*, Bernard Daries* or Guillaume Chaminade*.

In the infancy of my own religious order, the Marists, it was promised that Mary, the support of the church at its beginnings, would also be so at the end of time. It is perhaps important to note that many writers in the eighteenth and nineteenth centuries thought the end of time was at hand. Consequently, when they are speaking of the end of time, they mean their present time. They were convinced Mary had an active task at this present time. For them Mary is a model of apostolic mission. Whoever is called to the Society of Mary is taking part in her active mission to our time. He is to be present in the way she is present in our time. As Mary does good in the new-born church, without drawing attention to herself, Marists are to do good today by being unobtrusive. Effective but hidden, they are to weave a way into our time. So shall they, in some measure, make Mary present in the times in which they live.[12]

For the Fathers of the Second Vatican Council, too, Mary occupies a special place at the beginning of the church and likewise at the end of time. In the concluding chapter eight of the Constitution on the Church, *Lumen Gentium*, Mary is viewed as a sign of sure hope and consolation. She accompanied the church by her prayer at the beginning, and so continues to pray for it in heaven, until the whole family of peoples is happily gathered together in peace and love as the People of God (cf. *LG*, 69).

How the spiritual life of individuals and the community of

believers begins and grows is illuminated by Mary. In her also we see how it reaches completion.

With body and soul in heaven

The Catholic Church professes that Mary was taken body and soul into heaven. She found in God the completion of her entire existence. This mystery was already celebrated in the Eastern church from the fifth century, in fact after the Council of Ephesus. In the Roman Church the feast first appeared in the seventh century, but was only declared an article of faith by Pope Pius XII, on 1 November 1950.

We may ask: does this dogma not bestow on Mary the status of quasi-goddess? But one may also say: this mystery expresses how seriously God takes partnership with humankind. Because Mary lived all her life in interior union with Jesus, she is now entirely taken up into the divine life. 'All mine is yours, and you are mine' (Jn 17:11). God allows her to share in his divine and royal sovereignty to such an extent that she comes quite close to him. Is she not by the same token distanced from us men and women? Does the special blessedness which she has experienced not show just how different she is from us ?

The official statements about Mary do certainly need to be very carefully examined. The dogmas of faith, that Mary was conceived without original sin and that she has been taken into heaven body and soul, show no doubt that Mary was specially chosen by God. Their intention is also to emphasise that what has happened to her is promised to us as well. Of course, awareness of her position as specially chosen often arouses special veneration. In countless prayers, songs, places of pilgrimage, the devout veneration of Mary, Mother of Jesus Christ and Queen of Heaven, is expressed. Because she has a special place in her son's heart, many Christians call on her intercession and help in their cares and needs. Protestant Christians take exception to this kind of marian veneration and sometimes misunderstand it, as if it were adoration of Mary. It must, on the other hand, be emphasised that in healthy Catholic marian devotion, Mary always remains completely a human being, although she is one who has been in a special way taken hold of by the grace of God. What God can do with men and women shines out in Mary. It is permissible to express this in veneration and intercession.

A moderate marian devotion

Nevertheless, I would plead for moderation in marian devotion. As long as we remain at the level of venerating Mary and beseeching her intercession, we understand her as another person to whom we turn. What is more important is to look in the same direction as she does. It is better if we make her way of looking at things our own way, and try to live like her. The Constitutions of the Marist Society say: '... let them constantly try to breathe her spirit ... they must think as Mary, judge as Mary, feel and act as Mary in all things...' They are to express this, 'seeking not their own interests, but only those of Christ and Mary'[13]. Quite remarkably, in our community, called 'Society of Mary', and taking its name from Mary, no special form of marian devotion has ever developed. From the start it was much more important to live her life and to bring something of her presence to the time we are living in. Because of this a paradox has been noticed, that among all those congregations that refer to Mary, the Marists are the least marian with regard to special devotions to Mary, and the most marian in their effort to live out her spirit.[14] Without going into the truth of this statement in greater detail, let it be stressed that more important than any devotional veneration of Mary, is the effort to make her way of going about life our own. The greater thing is to allow Christ to grow in our lives in the way she did.

Image of a redeemed people

We should understand the official declarations about Mary more as promises of what we are all called to. What has happened to her is promised to all of us. The Spirit of God wants to bind himself to us deeply within. Those who let go to God totally and accept the offer of a binding partnership with him, are

entirely raised up by God, and virtually divine attributes become theirs. God has great plans for each human being: we are
to find in him the completion of our entire being. Mary shows us
clearly what happens when God dwells in a person, when Christ
becomes alive in a person, when the love of God arrives and is
accepted in all its purity in his creation. In Mary we see what
happens if a person does not keep God's blessing for herself, but
in all humble simplicity passes it on.

In Mary is revealed what people are capable of. We, in all our
brokenness, are still on the way to what has been completed in
her. We should trust her to intercede for us, that we may arrive
where she already is.

She is a sign of sure hope and compassion on our pilgrim
way through life. She will help us so that Christ may also be conceived and born in our lives, may grow to full stature and bear
fruit in the community of the church for the salvation of the
whole world.

CHAPTER TWO

The spiritual life in each one of us

The stages of the spiritual way covered by Mary are also under-gone by every Christian. As Mary conceived Jesus, so Christ must be conceived in each of us. Bearing him in her womb, she visited Elizabeth; every Christian is to become a bearer of Christ. She gave him birth in the stable at Bethlehem; so shall every Christian, in the context of his or her own life, bring Christ into the world. Jesus grew up in the house at Nazareth and he, the Christ, will grow from infancy to adulthood in every Christian. She accompanied her son right to the cross; every Christian must undergo a painful process of change, in order to attain new life.

What has been said here applies, not just to some specially chosen Christians, 'saints' as it were, nor only to people who have had special experiences of God, 'mystics', and not only to those whose lives are consecrated to God as priests or religious, but basically to all Christians. The Second Vatican Council em-phasised the call of all Christians to holiness. It pointed out that we are all together God's pilgrim people. All Christians are initi-ated into the deepest mystery of faith. We are all called through baptism to be God's children, called to put on Christ and be in him. We must emphasise this.

God speaks to people
As Mary was approached by God to serve in the work of salv-ation, so God approaches each person in his or her own way, not of course in a private revelation or through extraordinary phenomena such as locutions* etc., but mostly through the needs of the times, in order to serve for the salvation of the world. This appears already in the Old Testament, where God

spoke to Abraham, Isaac, Jacob, Moses and the prophets. This happened in an unparalleled fashion in Jesus Christ, God's definitive word to us people.

All founders of religious orders knew they were especially approached by God. Ignatius Loyola, Teresa of Avila*, John of the Cross*, to name only a few. Impelled by this call, they devoted all their energies to translating the call into reality.

God continually builds up the community of faith, but he begins by addressing the individual. Our modern, secularised world has discovered anew the individual, and this offers a good opportunity for the appreciation and development of the personal spiritual life of each one. The spiritual life begins with the individual, and then broadens out into the community of the faithful. Each one is personally led by God to benefit the whole.

Mary was called by God to a unique task, which included for her a quite special path in life. 'You have found favour with God. You will conceive and bear a son. He will be called the Son of the Most High' (Lk 1:30f). It is important for us to take in the magnitude and extent of this divine claim upon Mary, and not to dilute it, simply because we cannot imagine a virgin birth.

The human being as God's listener

God speaks to everyone and calls each one to the way of salvation for the good of all. However, we can only be aware of this call if we are quiet and listen to what is going on within us. It is also valuable to talk to others who are sensitive to the divine in their lives. This call can take root in us and eventually bear fruit. If we follow the call, we shall not be spared problems, but we shall be strengthened, so that we can master the problems that occur in connection with our call, come to full life and be helpful to others.

It is in fact just like the conception and birth of a human, and the stages of growth in a human life right up to maturity. Christian mysticism has made use of the concept of divine birth to characterise this process, but we are concerned with more than the birth of God in us. As Mary conceived and bore Christ, as she helped Christ to grow to full stature, so must we conceive Christ within ourselves, bring him into the world and allow him to grow to full maturity.

1. SENSITIVE TO THE DIVINE: THE VALUE OF STILLNESS

At the beginning of our spiritual way it is important to create room for stillness, so as to be able to become really aware of the divine call. God is devising plans of salvation for our time, and he is looking for people who are open to these plans. What happened once to Mary in historical circumstances, must now be fulfilled. Every Christian must bring God into the world again, as Mary did in her time and story.

Interior restlessness

In order to have the capacity to be aware of the call of God, there must be a still place in our life. It is precisely this stillness which is often missing today. The Danish religious philosopher, Sören Kierkegaard*, says: 'If I were a doctor and some one asked me what I thought might best be done, I would answer: First of all be silent! Help others to be silent!' Silence helps one to listen. Silence is not emptiness, but space for the Word. The sound of God is stillness. God appears to Elijah, not in the fire storm, but in the sound of a gentle breeze (cf. Kg 1:11-13). In silence there emerges a new sensitivity to the language of creation.

To what extent do we succeed in finding such quiet times? The hectic pace of work, family chores and even the recreation industry prevent us from really coming to rest. How then shall we keep a distance between us and daily matters, so as to see them in a wider context? The Jewish community created structures for this by introducing the Sabbath and giving it a theological basis: 'God rested on the seventh day, after he had finished all his work' (Gen 2:2). Not only are work and getting results precious, but rest is too, so as to see in the whole what lies behind the many details, but above all so as to be aware of God's effective action.

If we take time to be quiet, we notice first of all the noise of thoughts, drives and feelings going on within us. We become immediately conscious of our inability to be still. As people in our secularised world, we are in general terribly busy. We chase from one appointment to another, from one visit to another and rush from one piece of work to another. Our diary is full of arrangements. Being continually busy is the thing. People feel they count if they are continually called upon. Behind this hides the secret fear of failure. It is necessary to withdraw at intervals from this bustle of activity, if one does not want to be lost in superficiality. Edith Stein* acknowledges: 'We need times when we are silent and listen, and let the divine Word do its work in us.'[1] Christ also continually withdrew into stillness, in order to be alone with his Father. 'In the Lord's life the happiest hours were certainly in the quiet of the night, in solitary dialogue with the Father. They were a breathing space after intense activity.'[2]

St Bernard of Clairvaux urges us not to begrudge ourselves this quiet, so that our hearts will not harden. He recommends his erstwhile fellow monk, Pope Eugene III: 'I fear you are wedged into your numerous affairs, see no way out, and will consequently become hard … It were much cleverer to escape from some of your business from time to time, than to allow it to draw you on and bit by bit lead you to a point which you do not want to reach.'[3] The point we must not reach is the hardened heart, a heart 'which does not allow itself to be torn by remorse, or softened by devoted care, or moved by entreaty'. Bernard describes the hardened heart in striking fashion: 'It does not allow itself to be impressed by threats, and becomes harder under blows. It is ungrateful for favours and accepts no advice. It is insensitive to human behaviour, is indifferent to God, lets awareness of the past go by, lives careless in the present and looks not to the future. For the hard heart there is nothing worth remembering except offence taken, nothing important in the present, nothing to look for in the future or prepare for.'

The hardened heart results in a person being overextended in meaningless activity, and allowing the grace of God to fall flat. According to Bernard, one whose whole life is taken up with activity is by no means to be praised: 'What good to any one is a person who treats himself badly? Be good to yourself! I am not saying: Do that often. I am not saying: Do that all the time. I am saying: Do that at repeated intervals. Be for yourself what you are for all the others; or at least, be it after all the others.'

Healing stillness

In silence we confront the untruth and the half-truths of our life, our insecurities and bitterness. But in silence we also become aware of the healing, loving care of God. In silence we can again be aware of what is really always valid. We can be aware that we are always basically and unconditionally loved by God. Stillness is time to allow oneself to be loved again by God and to accept that love.

In a manner of speaking, God says to us: 'I always wanted to speak with you, but you never left me time. I always wanted to say: "I am there for you." But you were anxious. I always wanted to tell you: "Do not be afraid, for I am with you." But you did not believe me, but thought I was distant, absent. I wanted to speak to you all the more, but you would not let me speak out, because you are free to decide whether to listen to me or shut off. If you are ready to listen to my words, then I would like to tell you, "I have loved you with an everlasting love." My love remains the same from all eternity. Whether you turn to me or away from me, I love you.'

Quiet times allow us to experience again the liberating love of God. We can place ourselves at his call, and that releases us from preoccupation with earthly things. Then we are able to get involved in the radical changes of our time, and so be led forward.

People who commit themselves to times of stillness in their lives, radiate warmth and light in their surroundings. 'The more one is recollected in one's innermost soul, so much greater the radiance emanates from it, drawing others under its spell. All the more powerfully, too, does all free, spiritual behaviour bear the stamp of that personal uniqueness, which dwells in the innermost soul.'[4] As Mary was aware of the call of God, so can such people be conscious of God's call in our time.

The treasure of prayer

In silence the Word is conceived and born. Sören Kierkegaard says: 'According as my prayer became ever more devout and interior, so had I less and less to say. In the end I was completely silent. I became a listener. I had thought prayer was talking: I learned prayer is not simply being silent, but listening. Praying does not mean simply listening to oneself talking, but becoming still and waiting until one hears God.'

The Rule of the various religious orders urgently enjoins upon their members to make at least half an hour's meditation every day. Many take the day's gospel reading and, allowing its words speak to them, relate it to their own lives. Personally, for a long time now, I have been happy to stay with a simple word, which I allow to work on me. Such a word sometimes accompanies me over quite a while. So the sentence: 'What you lose for my sake, will be restored to you a hundred fold' (cf. Mk 10:29) accompanied me for a long time. Repetition helps to deepen prayer.

Simplifying one's prayer

Many people look for a spiritual word or let their spiritual director suggest one. Then they take this into the rhythm of their breathing. For example, take the short formula of prayer by Nikolaus von der Flüe*. You breathe out, saying to yourself the words 'Take me from myself' and while breathing in 'Make me for you'. Or inhale on the words 'Away from self', and exhale on 'Over to you'; then inhale on 'one with you', and exhale on 'new in you'; or quite simply 'me-you-one-new'.

Be helpful. Breathe in with the words:'You to me', and as you breathe out, say inwardly 'I to you'. Through this simplification, our heart is aroused. Those who regularly practice meditation are driven towards simplifying their prayer.

As long as we allow ourselves to be chased by thoughts and

moods continually streaming through our consciousness, our heart has small chance of practising contact with God. The busyness of our understanding often prevents us from letting the heart speak; prayer is more than anything a matter of the heart. Our heart comes in contact with the heart of God. At first that may seem like looking into emptiness. People who reach this stage often complain they cannot pray any more. They are wasting time; nothing happens. A hermit monk advises: 'Accept it humbly when you are bored and distracted ... If you are generous, you will gradually see God's world arising out of the darkness. You are already living in it, even though you do not yet know that. Believe me, those who have spoken enchanting, timeless words from the desert were no novices. Like you, they experienced dryness at the beginning.'

People who persevere, in spite of darkness, emptiness and the experience of doing nothing, will gradually discover a light glimmering in the darkness, find that in some mysterious way the apparent void has a heart. In the stillness we meet a living person who loves us and our world above all else, a person who has endured through all the darkness of the world and overcome it. According to Teresa of Avila, God coaxes us humans like a good shepherd, so gently that we are hardly aware of it. Gradually a person who prays discovers an ineradicable longing, driving him or her back to meditation, even when it seems to be empty.

Outward and inner silence are necessary, so that we can reach the ground of our heart. Of course this heart must first be shaken up, because it is often asleep. The Trappist monk, Andre Louf, writes: 'Today I have the impression I have carried prayer in my heart for years. But I did not know I had. It was like a spring that had been covered by a stone. At a certain moment Jesus took the stone away. Then the spring began to flow, and since then it is flowing all the time.'[5]

The Jesus Prayer
The Jesus Prayer is a good way of releasing the flow of this inner spring. A short set prayer is taken into the breathing rhythm and

constantly repeated. In the Eastern Church they like to use the formula 'Lord Jesus, have mercy on me.' People who pray regularly in this way find the prayer begins to fill out more and more unconsciously. Gradually the prayer continues of its own accord.[6] A similar set prayer formula can, of course, be formed by each person, e.g. 'My Jesus, mercy' or 'My God and my all'. It is also possible to give these prayers a marian form. As we breathe in we could pray 'Hail Mary', and 'Pray for us sinners' as we breathe out. In that case it is important the prayer be understood as centred upon Christ, not on Mary.

Contemplative Prayer

Some time ago I got to know and appreciate a simplified form of the Jesus Prayer through the contemplative exercises of Father Franz Jalics. In order to recollect oneself, he suggests directing awareness to the palms of the hands. He makes use of the fact that streams of energy flow between the hands. By directing our attention there we are interiorly alert and at the same time freed from distractions. The traditional way of clasping the hands in prayer, and also the position formerly prescribed by the rubrics for the priest to hold his hands outstretched facing each other, was born of such experience. But of course people no longer knew what the reason was for these prescriptions, which in the end only conveyed an external form, without anyone being able to give a reason for it. Anyone who tries will see how these positions serve recollection. So, attentive to your clasped hands, you become aware of breathing, and then with the breath say the name of Jesus – by itself, without any other prayer. As Jesus came down to us and surrendered everything for us on the cross, so we allow ourselves breathe out with the word 'Jesus'. And as God the Father raised Christ from the dead, we allow ourselves draw breath again with the word 'Christ'. Thus we echo 'Christ' as we inhale, and 'Jesus' as we exhale. At the end of a breath we can feel how this name echoes in our depths. We can feel how our whole stream of energy becomes more alive, from the head by way of the neck, heart and breast to the sexual centre. Listening to the inner sound of the name of Jesus Christ, we find a thought-free alertness and awareness. At the same time we are aware of his presence. The natural breath becomes thus a prime symbol of the loving breath of God, the Holy Spirit.

In contemplative prayer we allow Jesus to penetrate into the region of our unconscious and subconscious, and deliver it. Consequently he can free us from many faulty attitudes that we could never get rid of by ourselves. He wants to help us to get rid of wrong ways of treating our own bodies, which result, perhaps, in our being overweight. He wants to help us to a healthy relationship with our own sexuality, and to heal repression in that area. He will enable us to get on better in our emotional life, not to project onto other people and to forgive sincerely. In his loving presence our heart opens up, so that we are first of all more aware of his love and can accept it, and then can also pass on this love to the people we live with. Contemplation helps us to grow at every level of our humanity.

In all this, our awareness is in no way directed to ourselves but only to him, Christ our Lord. Naming his name encircles the image of his person. The consciousness of living in his presence grows in this way. Christ becomes the permanent companion and friend of our life. We can, with Teresa of Avila, describe prayer as 'a friendly meeting, where we are often alone together with the one whom we know loves us'.

In a quite unique way the artist Bernini represents in a sculpture how St Teresa of Avila, overcome by the divine, falls into an ecstasy and, as it were, conceives the divine within herself. The sculpture in the church of Santa Maria della Vittoria in Rome, shows Teresa wounded by the arrow of God's love shot by the angel of love. The saint is in this experience completely overpowered by the highest rapture of love. Divine light flows copiously over her. For this representation Bernini drew upon a place in Teresa's autobiography where she describes 'how an angel, small but very beautiful and with a radiant countenance, pierced her through to the very entrails with a long golden arrow, tipped with blazing fire'. And she added: 'It caused me pain, yet not bodily but spiritually, although the body also had its share. It was such a delicate caressing by God, that I ask him to allow anyone who thinks I am lying to be so cherished.'

Bernini succeeds marvellously in depicting this mystical experience, this being overpowered by the irresistible love of God. Here is a vivid representation of how the divine mystery is conceived within a person. When we look at the subsequent life of Teresa, we see how the divine bore fruit in her, the indescribable troubles she went through in founding the various convents of her community, and how she directed people to the spiritual way.

The first step on the spiritual path is the believer being receptive to the call of God in stillness and prayer, as Mary was. This may happen as at the annunciation. It may begin with a moment of fright, that God may be turning his love towards me, in spite of my wretchedness. Welcoming God may begin with a question, as it did for Mary. We are permitted to have questions for God, and to articulate them. Only then can we come to a fully personal decision, in which our understanding, will and feelings all take part.

2. EXPECTATION AND ENCOUNTER

Mary became pregnant by the Holy Spirit, and as she bore the mystery of God within her after she had conceived, so does each person bear a divine mystery within. Often we are not quite conscious of this ourselves.

Nurturing the sense of God

When a person has been interiorly awakened to a sense of God – for instance in the course of reflection or a personal retreat – he or she will be concerned to nurture relationship with God, for example, by practising regular meditation. Edith Stein* declares: 'One must live from one such time to the next, in order to be able to come back again. You cannot withdraw yourself from the judgement of a person with whom you live everyday.'[7] Although such times of prayer remain, perhaps, barren and empty, something begins to change in our life. 'We become more sensitive to what does or does not please. If we were previously by and large content with ourselves, now it will be different. We shall find out a great deal that is bad, and alter it in so far as we can. And we shall discover much that we cannot find beautiful and good, but which is difficult to change. Then we gradually become small and humble, patient and lenient with the splinter in the eye of the other, because the beam in our own has given someone else trouble.' People who pray discover with astonishment that in the course of time something has changed, just where they could not have effected anything themselves. Then they are thankful for the working of the Lord in their lives. They will return to the Lord, even when they do experience meditation time as barren and dry.

They discover longing, hunger for God within themselves, in the depth of their soul. Of course this longing often turns to other, superficial goals. But deep down, beneath this, there is hidden a longing for God. 'The soul is formed in the image of God. Therefore it cannot find rest in any other thing, except in its own form, impressed on it like a seal on a stamp.'[8] In some incomprehensible way God has created us in his image, as an image of God, and this creates in the ground of the soul an indestructible longing for him who has created us so.

Look at our longings

It can be good to look at the desires and expectations which declare themselves in us, without first censuring them, so as to learn how to deal with them well and constructively. We must concede that we have expectations no one can fulfil. Even the greatest success, the best examination result, the most wonderful holiday, cannot resolve our longing. It is just in really intense happenings that the longing for still more rises in us, wants to hold fast to the moment, or hopes for further increase.

People who try by themselves to still their longing, need more and more success, more pleasure, more caring, more love. And so they overtax themselves, and the others from whom they are looking for this love: they are expecting from another what finally only God can give.

It is, then, important for each of us to look at our disappointments: disappointments with people, our profession, our run of the mill life. We can then discover how good it is that no one can fulfil our expectations. That challenges us again to direct our longing towards God. Thus, through the very banality of our lives, we are kept watchful for God.

Many people cannot endure this unfulfilled yearning. They have to fill it up. It becomes obsessive. They feel anxiety facing this gap in their life that longing has uncovered, and which has become so strong that the hole must be covered up, no matter what. So it is good to locate unsatisfied needs and desires. They point us towards God. He alone is the fulfilment of our expectations.

God leads us into freedom

God alone can free us from the narrowness of our own imaginings, overcome us, grasp and change us. In prayer we can ask him to unleash such a movement within us.

The following prayer was formulated in the expectation someone had of God's effecting such a change:

Greatness of my God, shake me up.
Boundlessness of my God, free me.
Might of my God, vanquish me.
Holiness of my God, seize hold of me.
Spirit of my God, drive me on.
Will of my God, make use of me.
Wisdom of my God, lead me.
Essence of my God, sanctify me.
Mercy of my God, save me.
Light of my God, enlighten me.
Kindness of my God, bear with me.
Tenderness of my God, console me.
Peace of my God, fill me.
Life of my God, gladden me.
Love of my God, embrace me.

If we pray like that we are trusting in the greatness and power of God, bestowing his love upon us. We are trusting that the great promises of the Bible will be fulfilled in us too, that in our lives too water will spring up in the desert, and that in our relationships swords may be beaten into ploughshares.

If we hold out our lives to the Lord just as they are, with all their unfulfilled longings, then he will change us. Then the desert of our hearts will bloom, then in the midst of our emptiness and barrenness a spring will break through and exhilarate us. Yes, God himself will stop in at the stable of our life and come to dwell there. And his desire is to grow in us, as he grew in the womb of Mary, and to bring forth rich fruit.

Encounter

As Mary made her way, after the annunciation, to meet Elizabeth, so does every encounter with God thrust outwards and come to fruition in our meetings with people. Every genuine meeting with God drives us towards our fellow men and women. As Mary sought out Elizabeth because she thought she would find in her someone who understood, so it is important to find other men and women on the way of faith. They can encourage, inspire, help and correct us.

Together in faith.

It is very fortunate when in a marriage the couple can talk to each other about the religious dimension of their life. That is, of course, often not the case in a desirable way. Even in religious communities it can sometimes be difficult to arrive at a genuine religious conversation. But it is important to see the real value of prayer together and of faith exchange, and to do what we can to achieve it. Christ himself promised: '… if two of you agree on earth about anything they ask, it will be done for them by my Father in heaven. For where two or three are gathered in my name, there am I in the midst of them' (Mt 18:19-20). In common prayer we go beyond concentrating on ourselves, and become conscious of our common journey to God.

Bible and faith sharing groups

In Bible and faith sharing we allow ourselves to talk together about the word of God. Anyone who lives from faith has something to offer. Unfortunately, in our northern European countries there is still a widespread shyness among many Christians about carrying on a Bible exchange without a priest or some exegetical expert. But a Bible circle is not concerned with intellectually deciphering texts: all are invited to share what the word of God means to them and how they relate it to their lives. All Christians have, in virtue of their living in faith, a real faith competence.

For Bible sharing, those forms have proved their worth in which silence, listening to God's word, exchange of personal experience, intercession have a place and are connected. A group leader will see to it that all these elements appear. He/she can, for example, at the start invite the group into silence, and then, in a prayer, invite the Lord to be present among them. Then a participant can read out the Bible text, perhaps the gospel of the following Sunday. After further silence the participants are invited to repeat a word or a sentence of the gospel, without comment. Then they share with each other which word or sentence has especially spoken to them, or which text they found especially difficult and why. They may mention related experiences from their life. After this exchange, the group try to draw together what the word of God is saying to them, to what it is inviting or challenging them. The meeting can then close with intercessions together.

Difficulties can arise in Bible or faith sharing if the participants are not clear that common prayer is a different kind of prayer from private prayer. A person coming to a prayer circle in order to be silent will find the in-put of others disturbing. So it is important to take time for private prayer before, or apart from prayer in common or faith sharing. It is also important to avoid intellectualising the conversation. Bible or faith sharing are not for exchanging beautiful thoughts and insights. It is far more a matter of witnessing to personal faith and praying together to the Lord. The prayer can be misused, in order really to give the participants a sermon. Long-winded prayers are addressed to God, but are really aimed at the group. Personal witness in the 'I' form will avoid this mistake. It is important that we listen to God speaking in our hearts. If at a prayer meeting the participants become too strongly tied up in solving problems, the attitude of listening to God will be forgotten. It is also very important to bring the heart to listening to each other. Only thus will we be aware of what God perhaps wants to say to us through another or through the whole group. That attitude helps us to be sensitive to the divine mystery in others.

Sensitive to the mystery of God in others

When we live together from faith and talk about it, we can realise more deeply that our fellow human beings are also children of God, images of God, designed for partnership with God. All too often we measure our fellow men and women according to what they can do, and for what they are useful. We miss out on the deeper worth of others as persons. In faith we can become conscious of the mystery of God in others. In hope we perceive what is not yet, but will be. And in the power of love we assist the growth of the divine mystery in the other. Then we treat each other with deep respect and help one another to grow spiritually.

Thanks and praise

Alerted by faithful, hopeful and loving care for others, we discover the traces of God in our own life, even when the way God leads us runs somewhere else than we had imagined. That can move us to praise the ever greater God. We have always reason to praise God for the great things he works in us. We can praise him that we are images of God, children of God. We can praise him because he has called us to friendship, partnership with him. With Mary we can praise God for the great things he has done in us:

My soul glorifies the Lord,
and my spirit rejoices in God, my Saviour …
for he has showered his gifts upon me
and makes me ready in response.
He shatters my little world and leaves me poor before him.
He takes away from me all my dreams
and gives me more than I can hope or ask for.
He gives me the means to become free
and to burst through my limitations.
He breaks into my life
crosses out my plans,
leaves me yet again to think anew,
let go, be astonished, be still.
He exceeds my understanding
yet allows me guess at his mystery.
He gives me strength to dare
to build on him alone,
for in my life he shows himself the always Greater One.
He has granted me to recognise:
into a virgin being it is possible
for the mastery of God to break,
here and now.

If we, like Mary, accept the place God has designed for us in all simplicity and total thanksgiving, we too will become fruitful for others. As Mary awaited the birth of Jesus with joyful expectation, so must we also expect God will break more and more into our lives.

3. SPIRITUAL BREAKTHROUGH:
BIRTH OF GOD IN THE HUMAN BEING

Our life wants to bear fruit. What has grown within wants to become visible, wants to be incarnate in this world and its story. The history of spirituality has for that a great and deeply meaningful expression: the birth of God in humankind.

This expression 'birth of God' arouses ambiguous feelings

today. On the one hand it evokes fascination and on the other scepticism. Fascination because it holds out a promise of inner personal relationship with God. God is to be found, not only outside yourself, but also within. In the innermost recesses of your inner life, in the innermost chamber of the fortress of your soul, there God is at home. But the expression 'birth of God' also provokes scepticism: will this not encourage an esoteric piety? Will it not promote spiritual individualism?

In any case it is true that for most of us the entrance to this innermost region of the soul is firmly shut. It is covered in layers of dust. We are not conscious that the breakthrough to God also includes service in the mission of the community. The birth of God means a breakthrough to essentials: overcoming external legalistic piety and dogmatism, and an authentic life of faith, productive for the daily well being of the community.

The concept of the birth of God in us is particularly developed in the Christian mysticism of the Middle Ages, especially in Meister Eckart* and Tauler*, but is to be found in patristic writings as well, particularly in Origen*. There are also biblical inspirations which may be interpreted in this sense, especially in Paul and John the Evangelist.

In the Bible

The expression 'birth of God' does not appear anywhere in the Bible, but the Johannine* gospel and the writings of Paul speak of Christ being in us.

In Paul

Paul looks on his conversion as a way in which God revealed his son to him. 'Then God, who had specially chosen me while I was still in my mother's womb, called me through his grace and chose to reveal his son in me, so that I might preach the Good News about him to the pagans' (Gal 1:15-16). In his writings Paul witnesses many times to the enormous effect of this divine intervention in his life. God's action completely changed him. So in the letter to the Philippians he writes: 'As for the Law, I was a

Pharisee; as for working for religion, I was a persecutor of the church; as far as the Law can make you perfect, I was faultless. But because of Christ, I have come to consider all these advantages that I had as disadvantages. Not only that, but I believe nothing can happen that will outweigh the supreme advantage of knowing Christ Jesus my Lord. For this I have accepted the loss of everything, and I look on everything as so much rubbish if only I can have Christ, and be given a place in him' (Phil 3:5-8). What Paul has surrendered and now regards as rubbish, is his previous way of living as a Pharisee. From now on he strives to lay hold of Christ, as Christ has laid hold of him. So he sets out on a course of change, at the end of which he can say: 'I live now not with my own life but with the life of Christ who lives in me' (Gal 2:40).

In the same letter to the Galatians is to be found also the very beautiful passage in which Paul, without mentioning Mary by name, builds a bridge between her and us (cf. Gal 4:4-6). The twice repeated use of the expression 'God sent' is striking. God sent his Son, born of a woman. God sent his Son into our hearts, so that we can cry, Abba! Father! The first sending is that of the Son in the womb of Mary, the second sending that of the Spirit into our hearts. If we accept the Spirit of God with the same openness as Mary did, our life will become fruitful.

In John

In the gospel of John there is a whole theology of Christ's presence within us. As the Father lives and works in Christ, so does Christ live and work in us. Without the Father, Christ can effect nothing (cf. Jn 5:30). And without Christ we, his disciples, can do nothing (cf. Jn 15:5). 'Whoever remains in me, with me in him, bears fruit in plenty' (Jn 15:5). If anyone believes in Christ, 'from his breast shall flow fountains of living water' (Jn 7:38). And 'If anyone loves me he will keep my word, and my Father will love him, and we shall come to him and make our home with him' (Jn 14:23). Matchlessly concise, this is expressed in the words: 'I am in my Father and you in me and I in you' (Jn 14:20).

In the Christian mystics

What is touched on by Paul and John is further developed by the Fathers of the Church (by Origen and Gregory of Nyssa,* among others), and becomes for the Christian mystics of the Middle Ages (Angelus Silesius, Meister Eckhart, Tauler, Bernard of Clairvaux and many others) the principal theme of their creative work: the birth of God in the human being.

Meister Eckhart and Tauler distinguish three births of the Son of God: the birth of the Son from the Father, from all time; the birth of Jesus from the Virgin Mary in Bethlehem, in history; and finally the birth of the Son in the soul of each Christian.

What happened once historically through Mary, is to be fulfilled in every Christian. Every Christian is to bring God into the world again in his/her own time, as Mary did. It is not sufficient to reflect on the historic birth of Jesus in Bethlehem; it matters much more to make ready for the birth of God in ourselves.

'Thou shallst become Mary, and God be born of thee, if he will eternal blessedness on thee bestow.' In these words from the 'Angelic Wayfarer', Angelus Silesius expresses in poetic language the close connection between marian piety and mystical consciousness. For him, the birth of God in a human being is the summit of Christian existence. In Mary, who brought the historic Jesus into the world, we can see how we can prepare for the birth of God in our soul. In her we can learn how rightly to receive Christ within ourselves, to bring him into the world and to allow him grow to full stature within us.

For the messenger from Silesia, as Johannes Scheffler calls himself, restless humans are the real place of God's birth on earth. The way of salvation for each one consists of a continual progress in fulfilling the story of Jesus together with him. The eternal salvation of the individual depends on how far he goes with this process. Bethlehem is in him, and so is Golgotha. Thus he can say: 'Were Christ in Bethlehem a thousand times brought forth, and not in thee, forever lost shouldst thou still be!' For Angelus Silesius it comes down decisively to fulfilling the basic Christian mystery in one's own person.

'In the depth of the soul, in the spark of reason,' Meister Eckhart places the birth of God. 'In the purest, noblest, gentlest that the soul can offer, there must it be: in that deep silence, which no creature has ever succeeded in portraying.' 'God's Word, once born in the flesh, wills to be continually born to those who long for it.'

This birth of God is founded in baptism, where we are born again to new life. The primal message is promised to us: 'You are the beloved of God! You are my beloved son!' 'You are my beloved daughter !' 'You have I chosen.'

The Lord speaks to each of us, as it were :
I am there for you !
I am there when you are alone.
I am there when you are anxious and afraid.
I am there when you think all is over.
I am there when you are in despair and are sad.
I am there when someone hurts you.
I am there when you are ill and need help.
I am there when you cannot finish by yourself alone all you have to do.
I am there when your world is breaking up.
I am there when you come home again to me.
I am always there when you call to me.

And he says to us:
Fear not! I am there!
In the flicker of your hope and in the shadow of your anxiety, there I lay my promise: Fear not! I am there for you!
In the darkness of your past and in the uncertainty of your future
there I lay my promise: Fear not! I am there for you!
In the joy of your successes and the pain of your disappointments
there I lay my promise: Fear not! I am there for you!
In the narrowness of the everyday and the breadth of your dreams,

there I lay my promise: Fear not! I am there for you!
In your many abilities and in the limits of your gifts
there I lay my promise: Fear not! I am there for you!

Our ever-loving God also tells us, as it were :
I am there like the sun, which gives you warmth and joy.
I am there like a flame, never extinguished.
I am like a light, lighting up your way.
I am like a hand, held out to help.
I am like a heart, always beating for you.
I am like a friend, never leaving you in the lurch.

If we accept this message of God's loving care, our life will bear fruit. According to Meister Eckhart, every Christian who accepts the love of God and passes it on becomes like Mary, both Virgin and Mother: virgin, because totally open for God, and mother, because abundantly fruitful for others. Modifying Isaiah 7:14 we could say: Behold the virgin, the one open to God, will conceive and in her life ... or his ... bring God's Son into the world, and the fruit of this spiritual life will be: God with us. That a human being conceives God within is a fine thing, but that God should become fruitful in that man or woman is still better. True thanksgiving for the gifts of God consists in distributing them. Virginity is nothing of itself, if it does not come to fruition.

The Bible often speaks of this fertility: 'Whoever remains in me, with me in him, bears fruit in plenty' (Jn 15:5). We often try to become productive through our own efforts, but get no further than the work we have carried out. The result goes no further than our own little work. If, on the contrary, we rely wholly on God, interiorly lose ourselves and yet get on with the work, if we are both virgin and mother, then we shall bring fruit in plenty, some multiplied a hundred times, some a thousand, indeed times without number.

If we give our life over to God, it becomes exceedingly productive. May the experience of the empowering love of God enable us to respond to him with the strength of our love. May we hand our lives over to him, for he will take them up in the best possible way.

The great religious founder, Ignatius Loyola, lived out of this trust in God in all his apostolic labours. In his *Spiritual Exercises* he recommended the retreatant after praying through the exercises, to formulate a prayer of self-offering to God.

> Take all my freedom, Lord;
> accept the whole of my memory, understanding, and will.
> Whatever I have or hold comes to me from your bounty.
> I give it all back to you,
> surrender it all to the guidance of your will.
> Your grace and the love of you are wealth enough:
> give me but that, and I ask for nothing more.[9]

Only people who know that God has taken his home in them can make such a prayer. As long as a person retains a demonic image of God, and still feels God can intend to destroy his or her life, a prayer of that kind should not be made. Only unconditional trust in God entitles a person to make such a prayer.

This sort of prayer expresses the inner readiness of a retreatant to do everything God wants, whether it be tiresome and heavy going, promises success or not. The inner tension between prayer and action has to be maintained, so Ignatius advises: 'Trust in God as if all success depended on you and not on God. Take trouble as though everything depended on God and nothing on you.' The sentence is often turned around, but that eliminates the inner tension. We must act with such inner detachment from ourselves, that we expect everything from God. At the same time prayer must not be an excuse for not doing our best. Rather, prayer and action are in the best possible way mutually productive.

The more one is anchored in God, the more one is helpful to other people. In the great saints we can see the period when they were most inwardly attached to God was also the most fruitful in action. So, for example, St Teresa of Avila wrote the mystical work, *The Interior Castle*, at the very time she was seeing to various foundations of the Order, travelling in a horse drawn cart to and fro between Burgos and Seville, in the worst possible circumstances. Her inner union with God was the source of this rich productivity. Edith Stein expresses it, saying: 'I think that the more one is drawn up into God, the more one must go into the world, bearing the divine life there.'

Our human failures and shortcomings are in no way a hindrance to God's working. Just as Christ was born in the stable at Bethlehem, so will he come into the world in the stable of our lives. We should always reckon that we are only a stable, in which God is born. We are not a palace, ready to receive him. We do not deserve God's coming to us. His presence in us is an unearned gift. We are always simply a stable, in which there is plenty of dung and dirt. All the same, our life is where God is born. The definitive worth of our life does not depend on our outward successes, on career and recognition, but on the fact that God is living in us.

We need not emphasise our uncleanness. God appreciates us, and in spite of all, wants to dwell in us. With all our damage we should come before him. God accepts us the way we are now, not the way we should be or would like to be. So we should reckon on being accepted by him as we are now. Then it is possible for our life to grow.

4. GROWTH AND FRUITION

Christian life has to do with growth. In Luke 2:50 it says: 'And Jesus increased in wisdom, in stature, and in favour with God and men.' This brief reference accounts for the long years of Jesus' life at Nazareth. In Christian tradition Nazareth becomes a symbol with varied significance. In general Nazareth is connected with attention to a humble demeanour and a simple life style, but it also connects with esteem for manual work. For Charles de Foucauld* Nazareth is the most perfect way to follow the love of Jesus. He says: 'It is our professed aim to comprehend as perfectly as possible the life of our Lord Jesus Christ at Nazareth, on account of the great love of our Lord and the very great perfection that is to be found in following his love.[10]

For Peter Julian Eymard*, who was involved in the foundation of eucharistic communities in the nineteenth century, Nazareth became a symbol of eucharistic adoration. As Mary adored the divine mystery for thirty years in Nazareth, so did they want to adore Jesus in the eucharist. From there it is only a short step to seeing in Nazareth an image of the contemplative life. Mary lived thirty years long at Nazareth, always close to her divine son; so too should those who are called to contemplation, and are especially chosen, live in obscurity with Jesus.

Finally the mystery of Nazareth became a key in the process of genuine faith discernment. There is a saying ascribed to the Marist Founder, Jean Colin,* towards the end of his life: 'When I face a difficulty, I place myself in the house at Nazareth, and from there I see what I must do.'

Following upon these details from the history of the spiritual tradition of the mystery of Nazareth, we should like to direct our attention to another aspect of the mystery, namely, Nazareth as a symbol of spiritual growth.

Growth is an important topic in the Bible. Jesus has a whole series of parables in which he describes the growth of the king-dom of God. He compares it to a mustard seed that grows up into a great tree (cf. 4:30-32), or he compares our readiness to accept the word with seed falling on different kinds of ground, giving more or less fruitful results (cf. Mk 4:1-9).

As Christ grew, cared for by his mother, so must each person allow Christ to grow to maturity in his or her life.

Paul

Paul testifies in many ways to the growth of Christ in him. He often uses the image of growth … he wants to lay hold of Christ, as Christ has laid hold of him (cf. Phil 3:12f). He wants us to grow in everything until we have reached Christ (Eph 4:15). 'As every structure is aligned on him, all grow into one holy temple in the Lord; and you too, in him, are being built into a house where God lives in the Spirit' (Eph 2:21f). The whole creation waits with longing for God to reveal his sons. The whole creation groans until this very day in the act of giving birth … and we ourselves sigh in our hearts as we wait for the sons of God to be revealed (cf. Rom 8:23).

The more Christ grows in a Christian, so much the stronger will he or she be to bear the burdens of life. Paul testifies: 'I am certain of this: neither death nor life ... nothing that exists, nothing still to come, nor any power, or height or depth, nor any created thing, can ever come between us and the love of God made visible in Christ Jesus our Lord' (Rom 8:38f). Equipped with the might of God, we are able to serve others, as Christ did, and to perform saving actions in the world. '... it seems to me, God has put us apostles at the end of his parade, with the men sentenced to death ... here we are fools for the sake of Christ, while you are the learned men in Christ; we have no power, but you are influential; you are celebrities, we are nobodies' (1 Cor 4:9f). All the same, power radiates from the apostles, because they have broken the vicious circle of evil: 'When we are cursed, we answer with a blessing; when we are hounded, we put up with it; we are insulted and we answer politely' (1 Cor 4:12f).

There is a tremendous breadth in Paul's attitude, which crosses the boundaries of Jew and Gentile. 'I made myself a Jew to the Jews, to win the Jews; that is, I who am a subject of the Law made myself a subject of the Law to those who are subjects of the Law, to win those who are subjects of the Law ... To those who have no Law, I was free of the Law myself ... to win those who have no Law ... I made myself all things to all in order to save some at any cost' (1 Cor 9:19-23).

Christ grows to full stature in Paul. So finally he can say: 'I no longer live, but Christ lives in me' (Gal 2:20). Paul suffers the pangs of birth for the Galatians, as though they were his children, until Christ comes to fullness in them (cf. Gal 4:19).

Christian mysticism

When Christian mysticism speaks of the birth of God in people, this is only the beginning, as it were, of a long adventure on the way with Jesus. The child Jesus, who is born in us, is to grow and mature in us spiritually. Gregory of Nyssa expresses it strikingly:

'The child born in us is Jesus, who in everyone that accepts him, advances differently in age, wisdom and grace. For he is not the same in each person. According to the measure of grace in each one, he appears as a child, a youth and finally an adult.'

Romano Guardini* says that in every Christian, Christ lives his life anew, is first of all a child, and then matures until the believer comes of age as a Christian. Christ grows within the believer so that faith grows, love strengthens, the Christian becomes always more conscious of being a Christian, and lives ever more deeply and responsibly as a Christian.

The way of salvation of the believer follows a pattern of steadily accompanying Jesus in the story of his becoming. It is worth following up more closely this idea of the inner birth of God, the inner mystical growth and maturing of the believer. This story of becoming with Jesus reaches its full development on earth in a conscious, passionate and compassionate love, to be shown forth in eternity as the victorious love of the Risen One.

Our life: Growing awareness of ourselves as children of God
In the course of life all Christians should realise within themselves their own Christ-image. The way to becoming consciously a child of God is never straight forward. It always means working through the brokenness of our existence. That is why each one has different obstacles to overcome. The way of coming to accept being a child of God is always an odyssey of love as well.

At first there is perhaps only an inkling of relationship with God, as indicated by the twelve year old Jesus in the Temple: 'Did you not know, that I must be about my Father's business?' (Lk 2:49). At first we can only glimpse what a wonderful reality is hidden behind the kingdom of God. But we feel more and more that our life is growing, if we understand the divine message, 'You are my beloved son, my beloved daughter', as being addressed to us personally. Thus the inner feeling of being consciously a child of God can grow from glimpsing that relationship to articulating it expressly: 'Abba, Father!'

Admission into that spirit which goes with being a child of

God is never finished. It is entry into the way of life of the Son of God. It is a way into the freedom of the children of God. 'Everyone moved by the Spirit is a son of God. The spirit you received is not the spirit of slaves bringing fear into your lives again; it is the spirit of sons, and it makes us cry out, "Abba, Father!" The Spirit himself and our spirit bear united witness that we are children of God. And if we are children we are coheirs as well: heirs of God and coheirs with Christ... ' (Rom 8:14-17). What is said about being a child of God proves to be a never ending dynamic, coming to fruition in our own lives if we welcome the true divine reality with openness, as Mary did.

Then there grows also a new attitude of trust in God's guidance. Edith Stein witnesses to this many times in her letters. So she writes: 'It is basically a small, simple truth that I have to tell: how one can go about living in the hand of the Lord.' Or: 'Leave all concern for the future in God's hand and allow yourself to be by the Lord, just like a child. Then you can be sure you cannot miss the way.'

The more we live from the new experience of 'You are my beloved son, beloved daughter', the more our own life becomes the word which Almighty God proclaims.

Every new phase of growth in the spiritual life, from childhood to adolescence to young adulthood and then on to maturity, contains phases of purification. Growth entails clearing the ground of the soul of the many weeds which are thriving there. We shall go into the necessity for this clearance work in the next section, where we must speak of the thinking of St John of the Cross, the great master of the way of purification. In the spiritual life there is never question of destroying life, but always of more life.

The sacraments

In the community of the church, growth in the spiritual life always takes place essentially in the sacraments. We are born again in baptism to new life. We are promised that we are God's beloved children. In the power of this love our life can unfold.

We are freed from the spell of evil and can reach the perfection of our life by God's grace.

In the celebration of the eucharist we continually meet Christ. He comes to us inwardly and nourishes our life. As bread of life he wills to unite himself with us. As Mary received Christ within herself, we receive Christ into our life. As Mary went to Elizabeth bearing Christ in her womb, so can we bear to other people Christ at work within us.

If we feel we are becoming weak or falling on the way, he offers us his forgiving love in the sacrament of penance, and in the anointing of the sick his healing strength.

In spite of our weakness he sends us out into the world. In the sacrament of confirmation all Christians are armed for mission to the world. In the sacrament of marriage the couple are called and enabled to build up a Christian family. In the sacrament of priestly ordination the newly ordained is sent to preach the word of God, to minister the sacraments, to accompany people on the way of faith and to build up the Christian community.

Of course what has been given to us in the sacraments is to be carried through into the daily round. The love of God that we have experienced in the sacraments calls for a response in our lives.

Growing in love

Spiritual growth is shown above all as growth in love for God and people. Spiritual growth is finally growing in friendship with Christ. Many Christian mystics, such as Teresa of Avila, Mechthild of Magdeburg* or Gertrude the Great* describe this process of falling in love with Christ, which culminates in betrothal and marriage, but the reality of growth in the love of God is demonstrated by a true practice of love for one's neighbour.

Over and over again, Teresa of Avila exhorts her sisters to practice sisterly love. 'We cannot know whether we love God. But whether we love our neighbour, that is noticeable. The more you progress in that, the deeper your love for God.'[11] Love will be revealed in deeds. On that account Teresa encourages her sisters always to have time for the needs of others. 'Knowledge and talents are of no use if we also close up our heart to the needs of others.'

In like fashion Thérèse of Lisieux sings a hymn of praise to the great value of neighbourly love. 'Love of one's neighbour provided me with the key to my vocation. I understood that if the church is one body made up of many members, the most necessary and the noblest of them must not fail. I understood that it has one heart, and that this heart is glowing with love. I understood love alone is the driving power of the members, and were that to be extinguished the apostles would no longer proclaim the gospel, nor the martyrs dare to shed their blood. I understood love includes all vocations, that love is everything, embracing all times and places, because it is eternal.'[12]

In excess of joy at this recognition, she exclaims: 'Oh Jesus, my love, at last I have found my vocation. My calling is love. I have found my place in the bosom of the church and this place, Oh my God, you have given me: in the heart of the church, my mother, I will be love.'

Already drawn by suffering, she declares: 'Your love came to me from the days of my childhood. It grew in me. And now it has become an abyss, and I cannot measure its depth. Love draws love to itself.'

This love emboldens and enables people to make a tireless commitment to the things of God. The stronger the fire of love waxes, the more there grows a longing, 'to do great things for God'. The life of such people becomes to the utmost extent fruitful for their environment. Contemplative life calls forth the most lively activity. We only withdraw from the world at those moments when we are taken up into God's love, so that afterwards, strengthened by this experience, we can be present to our tasks more easily and better, according to God's will. In-depth meeting with God enables people to meet and to appreciate the world and others afresh. We have seen that already very clearly in the course of Teresa of Avila's life.

Love enables us to see what has to be done. *'Ama et fac, quod* *vis.'* If you are filled with love, it will inspire you to do what you should. Love becomes that inner teacher, of whom Augustine* speaks so wonderfully. According to him, the outer teacher only helps one to discover the inner teacher, and to follow him. Writing to his illegitimate son, Adeodatus, he says: 'I, Augustine, am not your teacher. Christ forbade his disciples to call him teacher in his lifetime. I forbid you to see the teacher in me.' And his son, Adeodatus, showed he had correctly understood his father's admonition when he answered: 'It has become clear to me that if a teacher says something true, he alone instructs us who by way of the external words informs us from his dwelling within us.' Not external teaching, but trust in the inner teacher is important to him. Entry by this way is certainly necessary today, so as to be able to find the route to the future. We shall only be able to tread that path if our inner growth is accompanied by prayer.

Accompanying prayer
Christian prayer tradition has a whole series of beautiful prayers based on the growth of Christ within us.

> Grow in me
> Grow in me, Lord Jesus,
> Grow in my spirit, in my heart,
> in my imagination, in my mind.
> Grow in me in your gentleness, in your purity,
> in your humility, your eagerness, your love.
> Grow in me to the praise of the Father,
> to the greater glory of God.
>
> Think in me, Jesus
> Think in me, Jesus,
> then will my thoughts be clear and radiant.
> Speak from me, Jesus,
> then will my speech be gentle and true.
> Work through me, Jesus,
> then will my deeds be upright,
> my work and rest be sanctified.

Fill my whole being,
permeate my whole nature through and through,
so that in me all may read your gracious love.

Jesus vivens in Maria:
Oh Jesus, living in Mary,
come and live in your servant,
in the spirit of your holiness,
in the fullness of your virtues,
in the perfection of your way,
in the truth of your virtues,
in the communion of your mysteries.
In your Spirit,
master conflicting powers within us,
to the glory of the Father. Amen

It is good to lay up for ourselves a treasure of prayers which have grown in our hearts. Then we can always go back to them, especially in times of dryness. Unfortunately, until now, scarcely any prayers applying to Jesus have found their way into the general prayer treasury of the church. Until this lack is remedied, everyone's inventiveness is challenged. The more room we make for Jesus in our own interior life, the more we allow him to grow within our very being, the more we shall be able to work effectively for others.

Fruitfulness: Catalysts in the world

Hidden presence
Christ often works in us in a hidden manner. He is present in us in such a secret way that often times we do not notice it. 'There stands among you, one unknown to you' (Jn 1:26). This word of the herald calling in the desert strikingly describes the manner of Christ's hidden presence in our time. We proclaim the hidden God in the right way, if we are simple when encountering others.

Simplicity

In our time, sensitive as it is to freedom and personal independence, an attitude of simplicity is especially important. In that
way the gospel of Jesus can take root in the heart of people, and
in different cultures. People who are not pushy are, by that very
fact, particularly helpful to others. They do not impose their personal style, but allow others their freedom. 'When God speaks to
a soul, he says a great deal in few words, so for example, hidden
and unknown in this world.'[13] John Claude Colin, the Marist
Founder, had a special feeling for the value of hidden service.
He sensed that, in the end, service without commotion is the
most effectual. 'Let us be small, let us be humble. If in the pulpit
we try to gain a victory and take people by storm, they react
against it and slip through our hands. We must win them by …
making ourselves very small …'[14] Colin turns away from every
sort of conspicuous behaviour in preaching, in the confessional
or in general pastoral practice. According to him, in our time
there is only one way of doing good: to work away, hidden and
unknown. Thereby we can, to some extent, begin a new church,
one characterised by simplicity, mercy and solidarity.

Just as Mary, in spite of being especially chosen, remained
always a simple maiden, so must anyone who wants to proclaim
the good news in our time, respond with simplicity to its needs.
Mary withdrew behind the saving work of Jesus, although she
played such a decisive role in it; so we Christians today must be
simple and unobtrusive, yet effective, while we leave the ulti-
mate decision to God. In this way we could heal the illness of
our time, and preach the mercy of God convincingly.

Respect for human freedom

The God who is at work in a broken world does not impose himself with power and might on human beings. God has given to
everyone freedom of personal decision. He respects this freedom. 'Human freedom cannot be broken by God's freedom,
switched off, but rather, as it were, overcome by stealth.'[15] God
will seek every way to win people from within themselves. If we

hear his word and follow it, our life will bear fruit. Like a fertile field, we will bear fruit thirty-fold, sixty, even a hundred-fold. If we are a fertile field for the word of God, like Mary, if we hear his word and follow it, we shall also be blessed, like Mary.

5. SUFFERING AND CHANGE

Growth takes place through phases of radical change, as old forms of life die off and new ones spring up. 'For anyone who wants to save his life will lose it; but anyone who loses his life for my sake, that one will save it'(Lk 9:24f). The grain of wheat must always fall again to the earth and die, in order to come to new life (cf. Jn 12:24).

On the way with Jesus we pass through phases of gloom, of not understanding him or God's leading. Whoever comes close to Jesus will not be spared the experience of being left without understanding. As Mary often did not understand Jesus, but nevertheless kept all the words of God in her heart, so the believer must learn to hold on to God's word, through phases of not understanding and of darkness. Mary stood by the cross and there felt totally forsaken, even experienced the darkness of God; so must we too undergo painful times of deep change, phases of darkened faith, even God's darkness. On the way we are asked to surrender much that had become dear to us: but that is how we reach new life.

The way of letting go is the way of the cross for our old, sinful nature divested of what was so valued until now, robbed of freedom, humiliated and, as it were, nailed down fast. It is quite understandable that we will stand on our guard against this change. But the more we learn to accept it, the more redeeming power will be released in us. As Jesus went on the way of suffering which our wickedness had demanded of him, so must we also learn to accept the suffering of our sinful human nature, that his love decrees for us.

Mary had to surrender her beloved son so that the work of the redemption might be fulfilled and we, too, must give up the beloved child of our life, whatever that may be, in order to receive it back at a higher point on the way.

The way of transformation according to John of the Cross
In order to attain true life, every Christian must undergo several
processes of change. All the great spiritual masters speak about
this in their own fashion. In John of the Cross we find a series of
images to illustrate the change from the old, sinful nature to the
renewed human being. There is the image of wood being
touched by fire, the theme of the exodus from Egypt and the
image of a vigil through the night.

Image: Wood in fire
John of the Cross describes, by the image of a log of wood burning in a fire, the passage through a dark night of the spirit that a
person must undergo. 'Fire, when applied to wood, first dries it
out, dispelling all moisture and making it give off any water it
contains. Then it gradually turns the wood black, makes it dark
and ugly, and even give off a nasty smell. By drying out the
wood, the fire begins to catch alight and expel all those ugly,
dark accidents which are contrary to fire. Finally, by heating and
enkindling it from without, the fire transforms the wood into itself and makes it as beautiful as it is itself. Once transformed, the
wood has only its weight and quantity, which is denser than the
fire. For it possesses the properties and performs the actions of
fire: it is dry and it dries; it is hot and it gives off heat; it is bril-
liant and it illumines; it is also light, much lighter than before. It
is the fire that produces all these properties in the wood.'[16]

The fire of God works in a similar fashion in the depth of the
soul, according to John of the Cross. First it expels ugliness from
the soul. Then it gives a person the impression of being worse
than before, more ugly and detestable, and thus purifies the person of all bad, perverse inclinations. Because these had become
so entwined with the core of the person, he or she did not realise
at first how much badness was there. That weakness and imperfection is now more clearly recognised than before. This is a kind
of purgatory for people.

In the process, God enflames people continually with a passionate longing for him. Although they must go on living in

darkness, there awakens in them a compelling desire, always impetuously reaching out towards God. The closeness of God is experienced more and more. Everything is now too congested for such people. They cannot stand themselves, and find nowhere in heaven or on earth where they can rest. In this spiritual night a person makes great interior progress, without being aware of it. The hollow place in human life is increasingly filled with the power of God.

When someone has come thus far, every situation can work out for the best. 'Like the bee that sucks honey from all the wild flowers and will not use them for anything else, the soul easily extracts the sweetness of love from all the things that happen to her.' Such people will become very enriching for their environment, since all their activity continually originates from the increase of love.

Image: Watching through the night
John of the Cross compares the whole spiritual process of change to a night watch, with its experience of three phases between the close of one day and daybreak on the next, beginning with twilight, when things disappear into obscurity, then midnight when everything is wrapped in darkness until the flush of dawn shows up everything in a new light. During that time a person has to go through many obscurities which serve to purify life, and in that way it is renewed.

Image: Exodus from Egypt
As the people of Israel were prisoners in Egypt, so are many people prisoners of their drives and passions. Release from obsessions in life is for them like the exodus from Egypt. Then they must wander through the desert for a long time until they come to transformation and a new life in the promised land.

With all these images John of the Cross describes a basic, stable structure: the experience of the wrong way, getting out of obsessions, the path through the desert leading to new life.

Point of departure: Problem of the false path

According to John of the Cross everyone experiences in the search for happiness in life the brokenness of human nature. As a rule people try to find happiness the wrong way. They create what they most want to avoid, come up before a block, manoeuvre their way down a blind alley. John says that happens because people are generally so dependent on worldly things, and these things hinder them from going further. He calls on those who are serious about following Jesus to free themselves from a slavish bondage to things.

Because of this call to detachment, John of the Cross is often reproached with despising the world. In reality, however, his position is far from devaluing the world. Things are not bad; indeed, they are well made by God. Human endeavour is created in human beings by God, and is not in itself bad. This striving should keep their hunger for God alive in people. The problem is that in our endeavours we are too easily content with second-best. Consequently, those affective powers become paralysed which were designed to impel us continually towards union with God. When our desires cling to certain things they obstruct this possibility. The result is that a person remains stuck at a certain level, and does not arrive at unfolding and flourishing.

John of the Cross illustrates this as the experience of Egypt, of inner imprisonment. If God wants to lead people out of this imprisonment, he lets them become conscious of their enslavement. They then feel cramped, unfulfilled and lacking in direction. They become increasingly uneasy about the uncomfortable position in which they find themselves, and from which they would like to be free. 'Desires weary and exhaust them. They are churned up and lashed, like water whipped up by a storm. They find no rest, so noisy are their inner drives ... Such people are totally ruined and destroyed.'

John describes the psychic defects of a life fixated on itself. 'The human soul becomes clouded when it depends on created things.' There is a chance of further development if a person recognises this problem of the false trail and is ready to about turn. Recognition of the false path and the experience of meaninglessness hides within itself the chance of further growth. The experience of barred exit and inner emptiness forces a person to look out for someone who can fill the void.

Jesus and the hungry heart

Many of the people whom Jesus met on their life's way were driven to him by their famished heart. Thus the tax-gatherer, Zacchaeus, permitted himself to take money out of the pockets of his own people for payment to the foreign Roman state, and to have a fine lifestyle himself. The people despised him, but in the depth of his heart he was burning with longing to be free of this muddle in his life. The meeting with Jesus (cf. Lk 19:1-10) lays this bare.

Andrew experienced in Jesus the longed-for Messiah, and immediately felt called to follow him. The councillor, Nicodemus, when he met Jesus, also felt himself filled with an incomprehensible longing for something greater. And so he came by night to Jesus, to find the road to a new life. The Samaritan woman, as she talked with Jesus at Jacob's well, also felt this longing grow within her. She yearned for the living water which, if you drank it, you would never again be thirsty, because within you a living spring would gush up, the water of eternal life (cf. Jn 4:14).

In many of the miracle accounts Jesus is at pains to awaken this desire in people. 'What do you want me to do for you?' Jesus wants to take people out of their lethargy and to awake in them the healing power of longing for a fulfilled life. Jesus is the bread of life, for which we finally hunger. Anyone who eats of this bread will expend his life for others.

Pushed forward by others, a notoriously sinful woman comes with a totally famished heart. Jesus turns to her intently, insightfully, annoying his Pharisee host by doing so. Jesus sees the essential goodness behind the woman's unusual gesture of love and awakes her to hopeful possibilities. Many are like her, their bruised and broken hearts already open to God. When we bring our broken heart to God then, by the very fact of doing so, we are straight away allowing new life to break in.

In the parable of the precious pearl, too, Jesus speaks of this burning desire in the human heart. When a man found a precious pearl, he sold everything he had and with great joy obtained that pearl. May we, too, retain a lively longing for God.

Is this desire for God not also present today in many people who are not content with striving after earthly aims? Even when we surrender ourselves to earthly objectives, and lose sight of our transcendent goals, the consequent experience of lacking something essential can arouse once more our longing for true life. May this inwardly uncomfortable situation impel us to break out of it!

*Departure: Release from the paralysis of fixation**
The way of liberation begins with our being ready to give up various fixations, obsessions, in our lives. It begins for us like the exodus from Egypt for the Israelites, with our having to get away from what we were accustomed to until now.

Those who get involved with God must leave behind their previous outlook and summon up the courage to risk taking this step. As soon as people get underway they go through a process of purification that frees them from various 'fixations', as Ferdinando Urbina translates the concept 'desire'. These fixations immobilise the affective powers, which remain stuck at some point in the person's development.[17]

Shattering these chains is for John of the Cross the principal act of liberation. He gives lively expression to it in the image of a bird that cannot fly away as long as it has not snapped the cord by which it is tethered.[18] It does not matter whether the cord is thick or thin, made of coarse yarn or of gold thread, or indeed is a devotional cord.

This process of release from everything that has become dear to us is a painful purification, but the night of cleansing from desire, which John of the Cross calls the Active Night of the Senses, is 'a happiness for the soul, and works much good in it.' In particular, the spiritual dynamism of a person, which has been blocked, is now freed up. So the 'Night of the Senses' does not at all mean an annihilation of the instinct for life, as Nietzsche* was so pleased to hold against Christians. It is rather a liberating therapy, serving the full release of a person's life-force and emotional richness.

Happy phase

Anyone who gets going on this road will now experience a time of happiness at being free, and will perhaps think that now, at last, the goal of the spiritual life has been reached. But we do not realise how strongly our action is impressed with our own power. We are not aware that we cannot of ourselves dig out the deepest roots of evil within us. God alone has access to that, and can cleanse a human being united to him. He does this through a further process of purification, the 'Dark Night of the Spirit'. God asks the person attached to him to undergo a tremendous purification, which reaches into the depths of a human being, and delivers it from spiritual fixations.

Deeper release

The exodus from Egypt of our lives sets in motion an all-embracing healing action. Paralysing attachments to certain religious ideas, devotional forms, methods of prayer, which were helpful for a long time, are gradually left behind, and the spiritual life can grow still further.

God will show people in search of him how many things they are dependent on, and will gradually help them to overcome these. He will educate a person to leave behind deeply ingrained images of God. He frees the person from the bonds of the past, still present in memory. He allows us to take leave of strivings after security, and so opens up to us the way to Christian hope. He frees us from making any decisions driven simply by emotion, and so opens the way to genuine Christian love. In a word, God educates people so that their higher powers, understanding, will and feeling, are increasingly directed towards the transcendent God. According to John of the Cross, people do not achieve that liberation from inclination and dependence simply by themselves. God intervenes in our life so as to effect the change.

Healing action of Jesus

Jesus continually called the people of his time to break out of their fixed notions and customs. He expresses this in the call to repentance, and also in parables, to open up to us new horizons. He bestows on sick people a presence that has already a healing character. Jesus has the ability to confront the un-integrated, and therefore especially feared parts of the human personality. In many miracle accounts he asks the sick person: 'Do you want to be healthy?', 'What do you want me to do for you?' With these questions he is appealing to the better and greater possibilities in people. He is inviting them to confront the dark shadows in their own lives and not to go on any longer living a lie.

Such an invitation quite often runs up against massive opposition. But in spite of this defensive mechanism, the questions remain as an offer and an invitation to healing. Jesus invites us to step up before him with all our darkness weighing over us. We are not to hand over to him only the beautiful and healthy side of ourselves, but also all that is dark, embarrassing, oppressive and shut off from life. He does not take it amiss if we have for a long time defended ourselves from appearing before him stark naked. Jesus invites us to confront the negative in our own life, so that the redeeming power of God can penetrate into these unhealthy regions of our lives.

The way through the desert: Liberation and transformation

The way through the desert effects an inner change in people, says John of the Cross. In the desert God will make a person submissive, in order to be able to free and transform him or her. It is therefore necessary to accept the desert. If we protect ourselves from it, we shall then become still more rigid. Because the sons of Israel were still thinking of the flesh pots of Egypt, they could not relish manna in the desert. The Israelites must slowly accustom themselves to the manna that God was giving them.

In the spiritual life this stage is characterised by the cross over from meditation to contemplation, from reflective consideration on truths of faith to a loving awareness of the reality of God. This, for John of the Cross, is crossing from the status of approaching adulthood to maturity.

Anxieties: Loss of our personal authority

A number of anxieties crop up at this stage, especially anxiety over losing control of one's own life. Indeed, God does deal with people at this point in such a special way that if they use their own power and capacities, they hinder rather than help the work of God in them. What people do of themselves only serves to disturb the work God is doing through their dryness.[19] To themselves they seem so helpless. They think they have gone wrong, and look for faults in their past. John of the Cross advises those who are experiencing this not to think too much, but 'to keep their souls in peace and relaxation, even when they think they are doing nothing'. He advises them above all 'to be lovingly and peacefully aware of God'. Without noticing how it happens, they will gradually be enflamed by love. A healed heart will be created, a heart of flesh in place of a heart of stone.

Of course this peaceful endurance of the desert is easier said than done. We would prefer to undertake everything possible to remedy this uncomfortable condition. But such activity would only be an obstacle to God's work. By way of this process we will gradually be led out of our own miserable way of knowing, our tepid love and scant taste for God. We will gradually be seized in the very depths of our soul, and indeed in our whole being.

The martyrdom of transformation

Getting on in the spiritual way involves a kind of martyrdom, as we are being transformed. Then we see more clearly how deeply we are eaten up by egoism at the very centre of our personality. We suddenly experience ourselves as proud, haughty, quarrelsome and angry. We are shocked at the garbage within. We feel unworthy of the love of God, and marvel that he could love us for a single moment. We often experience apparent desertion by God, and sometimes rejection by others.

During this restructuring of our lives we must overcome many frustrations. Quite often our understanding is shrouded in deep darkness, our will is dry, our memory empty. This results in interior fatigue, despondency and a feeling of being worthless. The whole process sounds like descriptions of burnout. We should be inclined to recommend spiritual or psychological counselling, a sabbatical year or simply a holiday.

All that might be good and valuable, but the Dark Night cannot be cured away. Rather must it cure us. How can the Dark Night of the soul be distinguished from psychic disintegration?

According to John of the Cross there are some clear criteria:
  – the darkness itself: the people concerned find relief in nothing, neither in God nor in earthly things, and they see through substitute remedies.
  – their life circles around God. Even while they are living in darkness they have a kind of nostalgia for God. They long for God and suffer from his absence.
  – they are powerless to change the situation.
  – results are slowly visible; perseverance in goodness, a new humility.
  – solidarity with the poor; hope against hope.

Such people are no longer intimidated in the face of power. The gift of wisdom begins to inform their actions. The change takes place without their really noticing it.[20]

A very impressive witness to the experience of the Dark Night and coping with it, is given by St Thérèse of Lisieux, who died as a young nun of twenty-five. Not long ago she was declared a Doctor of the Church* because she had shown how amid darkness of faith one can live trusting in the Lord. She writes:

God allowed the deepest darkness to invade my soul, so that

the sweetest thoughts of heaven were only an occasion of struggle and trouble. This test would not last for only a few days or weeks. It would only be extinguished at the hour determined by the good Lord, and this hour has not yet come. I would like to express what I feel, but really it seems impossible. A person must have walked through this dark tunnel to know how dark it is.

Thérèse can bring us to dialogue with the atheist within us, and so eventually with those who do not believe in God, and those who suffer from the contrariness of this life.

The old ego experiences this being taken hold of by God as a real way of the cross. In this manner, however, the imperfection of the soul will be burnt away, just as the wood is changed to fire by fire. On this road, which leads through so many dark places, only the lamp of blind faith is left to us.

A Holy Saturday experience

It is a real Holy Saturday experience. Jesus has really died. He has gone down into the deepest human need, down to the kingdom of the dead. It is good to sit in the church on Holy Saturday, before the empty tabernacle, and there reflect how it would be had everything come to an end with the death of Jesus, if there had been no resurrection. Christ endured total abandonment by God so that he might lead us to new life. On the day after Jesus' death, Mary and the disciples also lived through the darkness of God, the death of God.

We too can go down into the underworld of our life with Christ, because we know that from there he can draw up new life. Jesus descends into our aloneness, our chill and our rigidity. There, where we are cut off from life, he reaches us with his word of love. Christ descends into our shadows, into our unconscious, to release everything that is buried there. He goes down into the grave of our life, where many positive energies have been shut off. Many of us lead only a shadowy existence, dragging the dead around with us.

Let us hold out to him the blackest depths of our lives, so that he can transform them. This transformation is painful, like martyrdom. It is the distress of unregenerate human nature wanting to remain as it is. Only when that dies will new life appear. When the old ego dies, a great deal of energy will be released for others. The power of endless divine love can then stream out to the world.

*Stages of dying: Elisabeth Kübler-Ross**
In the course of her many conversations with dying people, Elisabeth Kübler-Ross has observed that they pass through various stages of maturing, phases of denial, aggression, bargaining, depression, before consent is possible.[21] What is true of dying people is also valid for coping with any life situation. Whenever we are required to let go, whether we have lost a dear one, or been injured, or must move on, we have to go through a similar process.[22]

Denial
Normally we are first of all stuck in denial for a longer or shorter time. As long as we cannot deal with the reality that we are going to have to bid farewell, it is best for us not to contemplate the situation. Denial is a psychological defence mechanism, helping us to survive in difficult situations, but as long as we suppress a part of reality we cannot arrive at fuller life. A great deal of psychic energy is lost, simply maintaining this suppression. If we give Christ a chance to speak to us quietly, we will soon observe what it is we are repressing. Perhaps that will arouse feelings of anger or despondency, but God speaks his promise, too: 'Do not be afraid for I have redeemed you; I have called you by your name, you are mine. Should you pass through the sea, I will be with you; or through rivers, they will not swallow you up. Should you walk through fire, you will not be scorched, and the flames will not burn you' (Is 43:2-4).

Anger

Our upbringing has taught us anger is bad, even sinful. In consequence we have been wont to hide anger from our friends and even from ourselves. But this is unhealthy and can lead to physical symptoms and to illness. Giving vent to anger constructively is a positive drive, helping us to see reality differently. It is a defensive stance against threatened loss. We should share this anger with Christ. He understands we are angry about a loss in our lives. Only thus will we become able to accept letting go, as the situation requires.

Bargaining

Before we get around to giving way, we usually begin to postpone the time for changing. We bargain. We want to establish conditions for changing something. In this way we make a lot of progress from the aggression phase, but we also reveal we have still a long way to go before reaching the end point.

Depression

Here now, in loss, we see the total eclipse of our life coming. We see that in loss we are being thrown back on the rock bottom of our life, and as long as we gaze into the darkness we remain stuck there. As soon as we gaze at the Lord in the midst of the darkness, he can point us to new life.

Consent

Here we begin to see the new life which was announced through loss. We can see where we have outgrown ourselves. We are even thankful, because we have grown just that bit more into the likeness of Christ.

Every therapeutic event has to pass through similar stages. Salvation and healing happen through the experience of the old nature dying. This process of change always leads through phases of darkness, and becomes a process of liberation from the constrictions of life. It is an unspectacular day by day path. The daily cross is everything that gets in the way of our plans, and substitutes for them the divine plans. The cross is there, where something is demanded of us requiring that we forego our own will, and accept the will of God. The cross means withdrawal from our own life and entry into the divine life. This new life becomes visible in the way the apostle Paul speaks of the cross.

Spirituality of the cross: Paul

A glance at Pauline theology shows how acceptance of the cross is a way of life. Paul is led, not to passive, cringing patience, but rather to a tireless engagement for the kingdom of God.

Bearing the burden

Following Christ leads Paul to respond to cursing with blessing, to persecution with prayer (cf 1 Cor 4:9-16). In this way he becomes dead to evil. It is an upright attitude that he learned from the crucified Christ. Nothing can separate him from the love of Christ (cf. Rom 8:35-39). Paul places every actual and every possible negative experience on life's weighing scales, and the love of Christ on the other scales, and he comes to the conviction that the love of God is stronger than all the negatives of the world. This is really the victory song of a person redeemed.

Tireless engagement

The sight of the cross leads Paul to tireless, unsparing engagement for the things of God. 'Although this outer man of ours may be falling into decay, the inner man is renewed day by day' (2 Cor 4:16).The inner person grows in the midst of threatening situations, and indeed by way of them. Through assimilation to the crucified Christ, new things can grow. Without readiness for the cross everything remains as it was.

Acceptance of one's own limitations

Paul also learns from Christ crucified to accept his own weaknesses. He suffers a 'sting of the flesh'. We do not know what he means by that, only that it must have been pretty burdensome for him, because he prayed three times over to be delivered from this 'angel of Satan'. But the Lord said to him: 'My grace is enough for you; my power is at its best in weakness' (2 Cor 12:9). The sight of the cross gives Paul courage, enables him to bear his burdens, reconciles him to his weakness.

6. RESURRECTION AND NEW MISSION

Through baptism we are, as Christians, taken up into the mystery of the death and resurrection. We are crucified with Christ, in order to be awakened with him. The victorious love of the Risen One bridges the two thousand years which separate us from him in time. Because of the resurrection event we can encounter him today in many ways: in the word of scripture, in the sacraments, especially the eucharist, in the community of the faithful, as well as in our own inner life. And so those who love him are with him across all the distances of time and space. They do not need anyone. They do not need anyone – as Lessing* hoped – to help them jump across the two thousand years' gap. They have already overcome it, in so far as they have made room for the love of Jesus in their life. This love effects the final change in our life. No special happening is necessary for that, no Mount Tabor. Faith in his life-giving presence is enough.

New life

The victorious love of the Risen One has brought the light of day to our hearts. 'It is the same God that said, "Let there be light shining out of darkness", who has shone in our minds to radiate the light of the knowledge of God's glory, the glory on the face of Christ' (2 Cor 4:5). In people who live from the Easter mystery, there is planted a germ of life that hides within itself a tremendous power for change. New life is given to them that can hardly ever again be lost. This experience causes Paul to say: 'I live no more, I, but Christ lives in me' (Gal 2:20). The Risen Christ had taken in hand the direction of his life.

In such people the inclinations and stirrings of Jesus are revealed, without the person concerned reflecting about it. They no longer have any special place or time of prayer, because they feel closely the presence of God in all things. They develop an ease in carrying out whatever is to be done according to God's right order. They are bearers of an inward peace which cannot be taken from them.

Outwardly, these people are no different from anyone else. But what is remarkable about them is their inner freedom, and it upsets some people. They do extraordinary things as though they were quite ordinary. They have the experience of things simply flowing towards them, without their having to reflect about it. They have knowledge which appears as and when needed.

Growing in faith

If we experience the overpowering, victorious love of God, an inner growth process will be released in us, similar to that which the disciples experienced on meeting the Risen Christ on the road to Emmaus.

With Jesus on the road to Emmaus

The story of the disciples going to Emmaus may illustrate for us how powerfully the divine love grows. In deep disappointment after the death of Jesus, the disciples leave the dread scene. Their hopes are buried in the tomb with him. Everything they had set the hopes of their lives on was shattered by his death. But they talk to each other about their disappointment. 'Our own hope had been that he would be the one to set Israel free' (Lk 24:21). This hope drained away with the death of Jesus. It is important for us to talk together about what moves or depresses us. Then we can understand that he, the Risen One, is with us in a hidden way. The anonymous Christ continuously accompanies our human story in every situation.

Then he begins to elucidate the scripture for us as he did for the disciples. When we relate our lives to the word of God, he begins to interpret them for us. Imperceptibly he sets our hearts on fire, until at last we recognise him in the breaking of bread, and we are newly empowered and armed for our mission.

A meeting with the Lord is already taking place where we help each other in our needs, is intensified if we bring our lives into dialogue with the word of God, and reaches its high point in the sacramental meetings with the Lord, especially in the eucharist.

Meeting of others with the Risen Lord

Just as their encounter with the Risen Christ changed his followers, so will that victorious love change us too. This will happen in accordance with the differences of character and circumstance of each person. We can see this very beautifully portrayed in the meetings with the Risen Christ described in the gospel of John.

Mary Magdalene

The meeting between the Risen Jesus and Mary of Magdala is without doubt one of the most moving and tender scenes and dialogues in John's gospel. Mary Magdalene is very devoted to Jesus and so she is the first to come to his tomb. She sees it is empty, and this heightens her grief. She thinks someone has removed the body and looks around for it, not suspecting that the Lord is much nearer than she thinks, that in fact he is alive. Hearing her name pronounced is enough to reveal him in the man she had presumed to be the gardener. Now she wants to hold on to him, in her way, but the Lord says to her: 'Do not cling to me, because I have not yet ascended to the Father. But go and find the brothers, and tell them I am ascending to my Father' (Jn 20:17). The risen Christ educates her to an independent faith; she is to overcome dependence and stand on her own feet.

Thomas

Quite different is the meeting with Thomas (cf. Jn 20:24-29). Thomas is a rather detached type of person. He was not with the disciples when the Lord appeared to them. He is not so very fond of community. In spite of their enthusiastic meeting with the Lord, he remains sceptical. He would like to form his own picture of the reality. 'Unless I see the holes that the nails made in his hands and can put my finger into the holes they made, and unless I can put my hand into his side, I refuse to believe' (Jn 20:25). Thomas is setting conditions for believing, but the Risen One commandingly waves these barriers aside. He goes up to Thomas in the midst of the disciples and invites him to overcome his reservations. 'Put your finger here; look, here are my hands. Give me your hand, put it into my side. Doubt no longer but believe' (Jn 20:27f).

Peter

Finally there is the meeting with Peter (Jn 21:1-19). We know more about him from the gospels. He is capable of great enthusiasm for Jesus, and is constantly active. He ventures to get Jesus to call out to him: 'Lord, if it is you, order me to come to you across the water' (Mt 14:28). At the transfiguration he wants to build three huts for Moses, Elijah and Jesus. He often promises more than he can fulfil. 'Even if all lose faith, I will not' (Mk 14:29). After Jesus has been taken prisoner he draws back in his anxiety and begins to curse and swear: 'I do not know the man you speak of' (Mk 14:71).

At a meeting with the Risen Jesus he is again in action. When the beloved disciple recognises him – 'It is the Lord!' – Peter straight off jumps in and swims over to Jesus. He confidently thinks he loves Jesus more than all the others.

This active Peter must learn to let go of the rudder, and to leave the steering of his life in the hands of the Lord. He must learn that love counts more than outward activity.

The Risen Lord and ourselves

Just as the risen Jesus took the disciples and Mary Magdalene beyond themselves, so he takes us beyond our way of seeing things. He leads us out into open spaces, makes plenty of room for us to stride about in. We leap over walls with him (cf. Ps 18:30). He helps us towards greater life, and will conduct us to the fullness of life.

In the saints this new life has come to full fruition. In them the inner world begins to show forth its light. Every saint is an original, because God has taken into account his or her irreplaceable uniqueness. Every saint is new, just as every human face is new. The saints are not copies but are the most refreshing originals that human history has ever yielded up. Each of us is called to this holiness. It is our true destiny.

The truth of the resurrection will be fulfilled in our life: it will reshape our life from within. What is decisive is the interior evidence of our life being completed in company with Christ. In that accompaniment grows the consciousness that he is living, because we ourselves are alive and are experiencing our life as being lived out with the living One.

Finding God in all things

We can find God here and now in all things. As Meister Eckhart says: 'If anyone thinks that in prayer, spiritual contemplation, a devout consecration brimming over with dedication, he is nearer to God than in the stable, what he really wants is to pin God down, throw a cloak over his head or hide him under a bench.' Such people are confining Christ to one way of meeting him. If people want to meet the real Christ, they will find him in all things: for them everything will suggest God, everything mirror God. 'People who are at rights with themselves are at rights everywhere and with everyone.' On the other hand, people who are not content with themselves will carry their discontent about everywhere. Those who live in inner peace find God everywhere.

We do not meet Christ only in prayer, but in work as well. In a special way we find him in the hungry and thirsty, those who lack the bare necessities. The great spiritual masters constantly emphasise that those who are praying must be ready to abandon devout contemplation, to go where their help is urgently required.

In the situation of life today, with all that now entails, we can still find God. He is revealing himself in what lies ahead of us,

the future in store for us. In every area of our life we must practice and strengthen our trust in God's loving guidance.

Building up the community of believers
Our life will be fruitful for our environment and for those
around us, by our receiving Christ within us as Mary did, and
by bringing him into the world and allowing him to grow to full
stature in us.

Christian faith is concerned first of all with individual
Christians, in the irreplaceable uniqueness of each one. It tells
them God loves and accepts them with an everlasting love, and
that they are called to bring to fruition the unique gifts of their
life. This begins with individuals but transcends them, and aims
finally at constituting a community of believers, indeed at re-
newing a whole world. What the individual contributes to the
whole, he or she receives back a thousand fold as a participator
in this great mission. 'A person's happiness is completed by sur-
rendering himself to something greater than himself' (Teilhard
de Chardin*).

If we try to live like Mary, to think, judge and act like her, we
shall also begin by working for the good of the community of believers. We shall then receive the gifts God has given us and
thank him for them. We will accept his love, and endeavour to
respond to them accordingly. We will contribute to the well-
being of the whole body, in only a modest way perhaps, but
energetically and eagerly.

The Constitutions of the Society of Mary outline attitudes
which follow if Marists seek to live from the spirit of Mary: not
to look to one's own interests, but to those of Jesus and Mary; to
be free of self-centred behaviour; to cultivate an unpretentious
lifestyle, practice simplicity, humility and singleness of heart.
'Acting always with such great poverty, humility and modesty,
simplicity of heart, and unconcern for vanity and worldly ambi-
tion, and moreover so combining a love of solitude and silence
and the practice of hidden virtues with works of zeal, that even
though they must undertake the various ministries helpful to

the salvation of souls, they seem to be unknown and indeed even hidden in this world.'[23]

The exhortation to humility and the cultivation of hidden virtues does not mean, of course, that they are to hide their light under a bushel. They are rather to accept the gifts God has given them and to deploy them for the good of the community. The Founder of the Society, Father John Claude Colin, expressed this very beautifully: 'How I like that prayer: "Lord, do great things through me." Some people may say, "But that is pride!", but on the contrary, I say it is humility. For I am nothing and God made the world from nothing. By this prayer I acknowledge my nothingness, and the almighty power of God.'[24]

Humility and magnanimity – greatness of heart – belong closely together. Just at the moment when I recognise my unworthiness, the might of God is disclosed to me. I recognise the rich gifts he has bestowed on me, and I feel the responsibility following from these gifts. I become conscious that only with God's help can I be aware of the responsibility passed on to me.

Two or three

In the Bible it is often promised that great things happen where two or three are gathered in the name of Jesus. Where they are gathered in his name to ask for something, he will do it. 'Where two or three gather in my name, there am I in the midst of them' (Mt 18:20).

We may ask: 'What are two or three? What can they effect, especially if one is blind, another deaf and a third lame?' But one can look at it another way. The blind person can let the deaf one know what he has heard, the deaf person one can lead the blind one, and both together they can carry the lame one. Together we are more than the sum of the individuals. Together as believers we have the Lord in our midst. Together we can bring about the kingdom of God.

Jesus sends out his disciples two by two to proclaim the good news. He collects a group of disciples around him, to take the message of the kingdom of God into the whole world. In the community of believers he is present as the Lord, still living and present. The community of believers is the body of Christ, with Christ as its head. There too will Christ be received, be born and grow to full stature.

CHAPTER THREE

In the Community of the Faith

The stages of the spiritual life we have discerned in Mary, and that individual Christians experience on their spiritual journey, are also stages of growth in the faith community. The community of believers must also receive God's word and cultivate it together in their meetings before they can pass on the word to those who do not believe in Christ, or no longer do so. The community must also go through a process of radical change, and so come to new life.

In the concluding chapter of the *Constitution on the Church* (*Lumen Gentium* 53), the Second Vatican Council emphasised that Mary is a type, a basic image of the church. Just as she, Virgin Mother, brought Christ into the world, so we, a community of believers, must be receptive to God's word, and fruitful for others.

The formation of the community of believers has experienced various stages of growth, and the process is never finally concluded. The church is continuously re-established by people who are together open to the call of God, allowing themselves to be totally formed by his call. The church is built up by people who let faith shape their lives, and whose individual charisms combine to the good of the whole.

Gathering around the Lord – Proclaiming the kingdom of God
In the Bible we can already see different phases in the emergence of the church. There is already a beginning of church where Jesus gathers people around himself through his preaching and healing activity. He assembles a community of people who are looking forward to the coming of the kingdom of God, and

already feel it's enduring presence. Of course this collective movement comes to a rude end when Jesus, still a young man, must die a cruel death on the cross. In his farewell talk to the disciples, he prepares them for the time after his death, leaving them many precious sayings to console them. 'I am going now to my Father... You will mourn now... but I will not leave you as orphans. I am sending you the Comforter, the Holy Spirit, who will lead you into all truth... Let not your hearts be troubled! In my Father's house there are many rooms. Remain with me, as the branch remains attached to the vine. I will not call you servants any more, I call you friends' (cf. Jn 14-17).

Death and resurrection of Jesus

In the midst of outward collapse, the new movement around the glorified One is already showing signs of life. That is why John the Evangelist in his gospel let fall those words of the Lord: 'If I am raised up over the earth, I will draw all to me' (Jn 12:32). Cross and resurrection coincide in a mysterious way for John. When Jesus is dying he breathes out his Spirit. This Spirit belongs to the whole world. His saving work is complete, so the last words of Jesus recorded in John's gospel are 'It is accomplished' (Jn 19:30).

John then describes in remarkable detail how the side of Jesus was opened with a lance and blood and water flowed out. The fathers of the church very early on saw here a symbol of the foundation of the church. As Eve was taken from Adam's rib, so the church issued from the Lord's side. The heart of the Risen One remains open to the end of time. The wounds of Jesus will not be erased by the resurrection, but they are transfigured. In them is revealed the boundless love of God for us.

According to John, the Risen Jesus sends the Holy Spirit to his own, at once, upon Easter Day. At his first meeting with the disciples he says: 'Receive the Holy Spirit! Whose sins you forgive, they are forgiven; to whom you refuse forgiveness, to them it is refused' (Jn 20:22). For John, resurrection and sending the Spirit coincide.

The Sending of the Spirit

According to Luke's version a further important divine impulse was necessary beyond the resurrection to enable the disciples to go out into the whole world: the sending of the Spirit. With this decisive event in the divinely appointed group, Luke begins the Acts of the Apostles. The disciples had locked themselves into the supper room; then the Spirit of Pentecost sprang open the doors of their life and enabled them to go out into the world and proclaim the good news. In a real and comprehensive sense, this was the hour of the church's birth.

As Mary conceived by the Holy Spirit, she is now at hand when the young church is conceived by the power of the Spirit and comes to birth. Subsequently the church grows outwardly in numbers and inwardly through the action of a variety of charisms.

Let us now reflect on the various phases of the church's conception and birth, its growth, its path through cross and suffering to maturity and fullness.

1. THE COMMUNITY OF FAITH AT PRAYER: RECEPTIVE TO THE SPIRIT OF GOD

Mary was receptive to the call of God which she received at the annunciation; individual Christians become receptive to the call of God in so far as they create a place of stillness in their lives. The community of believers also requires a receptive atmosphere. It creates this by calling its members together into a community of prayer.

Christian life as a community of faith begins with believers gathering to declare together their common origin from God, to pray together for the coming of the Spirit, as did Mary and the apostles. The days between the ascension of Christ and Pentecost are a preparation for the birth of the church in the power of the Spirit. As Mary bore Christ for nine months in her womb, so do the apostles pray with her for nine days for the coming of the Spirit.

Whenever we pray together, we should be aware of the

promise of the Lord regarding the power of common prayer: '…
if two of you on earth agree to ask anything at all, it will be
granted to you by my Father in heaven. For where two or three
meet in my name, I shall be there with them' (Mt 18:19-20).

Between Ascension and Pentecost

The period between the ascension of Christ and Pentecost, strikingly emphasises a state of incompletion between the 'already'
and the 'not yet'. Something decisively new has already begun,
but it is not yet perfected. Christ has returned to the Father. He
has promised to send the Spirit to his disciples, but the Spirit has
not yet been poured out on them. The disciples have been forti-
fied by the Easter experience, Christ remaining close to them
after his suffering and death, but they are not yet empowered to
act in his name. They have gathered behind locked doors for fear
of the Jewish authorities and are praying together for the coming of the Holy Spirit. The between-times of uncertainty is a time
of prayer.

The disciples and Mary look back to past experiences, how
Jesus had gathered them together by his preaching of the kingdom of God, had called them to follow him, and how they had
found the fulfilment of their lives in following him. They remembered how he had bestowed a healing presence on many,
had thought of himself as 'friend of publicans and sinners' and
thereby had run into ceaseless conflict with the Pharisees. They
thought of how he had nevertheless remained true to his way,
right to the frightful death on the cross. They thought back to the
unexpected and astonishing experience of his meeting them as
the Risen Lord, and his gathering together again the dispersed
group of disciples.

But they were also looking towards the future. They had
heard the order Jesus had given them: 'Go out and teach all peoples and make everyone a disciple of mine; baptise them in the
name of the Father and of the Son and of the Holy Spirit … be
sure: I am with you all days, even to the end of the world' (Mt
28:19f). They had already received their instructions, but they
had no idea how they could be carried out.

This interval is for them a time of waiting for God's Spirit, and for his leading. It is a time of waiting together, a time of retirement and of prayer.

Today

We too experience similar between-times, full of uncertainty, cares and questions, challenging our courage, daring and trust. Every period really has its share of these ambivalent between-stages. Something has begun, but is not yet complete. Alfred Delp* expressed this very strongly in the diary he wrote at the concentration camp in Berlin – Ploetzensee. In the days between his arrest and execution, he went through a series of pentecostal experiences leading to a great prayer of freedom, in which he could articulate all the boundless longing of his heart, as well as the shattering misery of his existence.

In prayer together, we put into words the cares and needs of our common journey. We are first of all a community of prayer and of eucharistic celebration, before we can be a visible community sent out, a missionary church. Christian life is extremely forceful when it works from inwards out. The Christian community is powerful if its members live out of a deep faith, if indeed they penetrate to the mystical heart of Christianity and live from there. We have already noted Rahner's strikingly prophetic word: 'The Christian of tomorrow will be a mystic, one who has experienced God, or he will not be a Christian at all.'[1] In all spiritual groups wanting to live more intensively what being church means, and especially in the various religious orders, regular common prayer and particularly celebration of the eucharist together are always considered to be central. Common breaking of bread, hearing together God's word and giving thanks together for his mighty deeds, have been practised from the beginning of the church, wherever Christians foregathered. But common prayer must continue into daily life.

2. A CHURCH OF BROTHERS AND SISTERS
… AWAITING THE ONE WHO IS COMING

Expectation

Mary became pregnant after the annunciation and was waiting for the birth of Christ; during the interval between the ascension and Pentecost the apostles were waiting for the coming of the Holy Spirit. The church also is essentially an expectant community.

After the Spirit of God had descended on the apostles, they eagerly proclaimed the message of Christ, crucified and risen. At the same time, the young church was awaiting, full of confident hope, the imminent return of the Lord. At first they thought this return was so near at hand that many would experience it in their own life time. So they did not want to burden their lives with earthly things any more. Instead, they sold everything and lived in great simplicity. They devoted all their energies to preparing for the return of the Lord. This expectation gave a peculiar intensity and power to their lives.

Soon, however, they were forced to realise the period before the return of the Lord was going to be much longer than they had thought. Many got tired and grew weary of religious zeal. It was the apostle Paul who helped the Christian body to master this crisis. He made clear that Christians are called during this time to win the whole world to Christ with missionary ardour.

In the course of the centuries, and especially since the recognition of Christianity as the state religion in the Roman Empire, the sense of the imminent return of the Lord was increasingly lost. But the more the eschatological* spur was lost, the more the faith became domesticated. It is assuredly important in our time to renew the expectation of the coming Lord. We Christians are and remain an expectant community, a community of hope.

Every Advent the church places this reality before us again. She lays before us many texts from the Old Testament, especially from the prophet Isaiah. Many generations have awaited salvation and redemption. They have waited for the time when the wolf and the lamb will live together in peace, when swords will be beaten into ploughshares, Isaiah's tree-stumps bring forth a new shoot.

These texts should not take us back to a past when the Redeemer had not yet come. Rather do they help us today, two thousand years after the coming of the Lord, to be hopeful, expectant people, crying out: 'Maranatha! Come, Lord Jesus! Come soon!'

The church is a waiting community. It is a good thing to talk together about our expectations and hopes as Christians, about our hope of greater community, our hope for peace and justice in the world, for reconciliation among people.

Meeting

How happy Mary was to find in Elizabeth someone with whom she could speak about the divine mystery in her life; it is good for us too to build a faith community of mutual understanding. When the apostles were assembled together with Mary in the upper room, they did not pray only for the coming of the Spirit, but also shared their life with one another. Yes, they even began to make community decisions, trusting in the power of the Spirit. Thus, they took some counsel about the future composition of the group of Twelve, and finally drew lots, seeking God's choice.

A church of brothers and sisters

The young church experienced itself as a company of brothers and sisters. All who believe in Christ are brothers and sisters. Jesus, when he was on earth, had himself spoken of this new relationship. When told his mother and brothers had arrived and were asking for him, he said: 'Here are my mother and my brothers. Anyone who does the will of God, that person is my brother and sister and mother' (Mk 3:35).

As one family, this community shared out the necessities of life among themselves. 'The whole group was united, heart and soul; no one claimed for his own use anything that he had, as everything they owned was held in common' (Acts 4:32). As emphasised by Luke, unity was the dominant note. This fundamental unity made it possible to bear tensions which certainly existed within the young church. Conflicts were so sharp that Paul found it necessary to confront Peter, the leader of the church, to his face. Such conflicts could be borne because all the participants knew they were held together by the Lord.

Paul developed a theology of the church as the Body of Christ, with Christ as its head and with many members, each having its task for the good of the whole (e.g. 1 Cor 12:12-27). This image grew out of his conversion experience before Damascus. There he knew a voice from heaven was addressing him: 'Saul, Saul, why are you persecuting me?' (Acts 9:4). By persecuting Christians, he was persecuting Christ. Thus he developed a theology based on the identification of Christ and Christians.

The community of believers is the Mystical Body of Christ. Within it each one has a special task that serves the whole body, and therefore all are equally valuable in ensuring its ability to function. All Christians experience themselves as part of one great communion, having the Lord in their midst. 'Where two or three are gathered together in my name, there am I in their midst' (Mt 18:20). Anyone entrusted with a task of leadership in the church is not placed over his fellow believers, but should be like Christ, the servant of the others. This service consists above all in developing for the good of all the various charisms existing within the community.

In the course of time all the charisms became concentrated on the leader, and the people of God became, to a considerable extent, deprived of looking after their affairs. Even at the beginning of the twentieth century Leo XIII could still write: 'It is quite evident that there are two groups in the Church, the Shepherds and the Flock, in other words, the Leader and the People. The first have the duty of teaching and leading the people in their life, and of setting out for them the necessary rules. The others have the duty of submitting to the first, of listening to them and showing them honour.'[2]

The Second Vatican Council brought about a fundamental change in this situation. It strongly emphasised the fundamental equality of all Christians based upon their baptism. The clergy are no longer the focus point around which the People of God are defined. The baptised are themselves that focus point. Priests and laity together form a single pilgrim people. From Mary, the image of the church, we can learn to build up a community together, where people listen to each other, share with each other, a community of equals with Christ in the midst.

The witness of a sisterly, brotherly community of believers is especially important in our modern, secularised world. We have indeed discovered, in a positive way, the value of the individual, but are at the same time in danger of falling into individualism, and of losing the sense of community. We must strengthen our awareness of the need to devote ourselves to something greater than our own selves.

We must not, however, restrict ourselves only to the company of those who walk with us in faith, but seek much further, to build community with all. The church is surely a 'Sacrament of Salvation for the whole world' (*Lumen Gentium* 1).

3. MISSIONARY CHURCH: BIRTH OF THE CHURCH THROUGH THE FIRE OF THE HOLY SPIRIT

The church does not exist for its own sake, but for the coming of the kingdom of God. In the full sense, the church is only there when it is effective beyond itself. It belongs to the essence of the church to open out to those who do not believe or who can no longer believe. If the church of Jesus Christ is to remain true to itself, it must always be missionary and bestir itself to proclaim the good news to all people at all times.

Pentecost event – birthday of the church
The happenings at Pentecost were the birthday celebration of this missionary church. Just as Mary gave birth to Jesus at Bethlehem, and as every Christian must give birth to God in his or her soul, so is the church, as a missionary body, born by the

power of the Spirit. The doors behind which the disciples had locked themselves for fear of the Jewish authorities, are burst open by the Holy Spirit. He makes courageous apostles out of timorous disciples, and enables them to go out into the whole world in full power.

Fire

The coming of the Spirit is described by Luke as a tremendous event. The Spirit of God comes in storm and fire, signs of primitive, untamable power. With indomitable energy the Spirit of God descends upon each individual and fills the whole house. It comes on each one in his or her individuality and uniqueness, and at the same time creates around the whole group a Spirit filled atmosphere (cf. Acts 2:1-4).

God is for us fire and flame. Whoever draws near to that fire is changed. The experience of mystical breakthrough has been expressed many times through the image of fire. For example, Pascal* used to carry about with him, stitched into the lining of his coat, a piece of paper on which he had written down his overwhelming experience of God on the night of 23/24 November 1654. 'From 11.30 p.m. to 12.30 a.m. Fire, Fire, Fire! God of Abraham, God of Isaac, God of Jacob, not of the philosophers! Certainty, certainty, inner experience. Joy, Peace!'[3] In the image of fire, Pascal is describing his deep mystical experience, which gave him new vitality after being driven hither and thither for years.

For John of the Cross fire becomes a central image to describe what goes on between God and human beings. A person who draws near to this fire is at first dried out like wood, then set alight and finally is more and more changed into fire.

On the day of Pentecost this fire seized not only an individual but a whole community. The love of God set the disciples on fire and enabled them to go out into the whole world and proclaim the good news of Christ.

In different languages

Through God's Spirit the disciples were enabled to speak in such a way that people of the most varied nationality and provenance could understand them (Acts 2:5-13). According to the Book of Genesis, it was on account of overweening human pride that people could no longer understand each other. They wanted to build a tower that would reach heaven, so as to equal God. This arrogance led to their being divided among themselves, to such an extent that for all their own efforts to find ways to each other, they got lost in a thicket of self-centredness and human projection.

God's Spirit makes possible what seems impossible. He strides over walls and frontiers, behind which we have barricaded ourselves. He is creative and takes initiatives. He wants to reach everyone. He builds across the chasms of our life, and so enables us once more to find ways to each other. He respects our freedom, but at the same time moves in such a way as to win us from within ourselves.

The Spirit of God urges the disciples to proclaim the gospel to the whole world. Whoever is filled with this Spirit will grow in missionary zeal. Paul witnesses to the inner pressure to declare: 'Necessity is laid upon me. Woe to me if I do not preach the gospel' (1 Cor 9:16). An astonishing frankness and universal openness are the result of these urgings of the Spirit, so that Paul becomes the great apostle of the heathens. But all the other apostles acknowledge they too are driven by the Spirit of God: 'We cannot but speak of what we have seen and heard' (Acts 4:20).

The early church: a model

In the early church it is clear what a small group of Christians can achieve if they set to work with conviction and enthusiasm. They began as the tiny mustard seed and, with the help of God's Spirit, they became a considerable tree. In the early church we see the mystery of modest beginnings, but also what the power of God can do with them.

The early church was still living out of the consciousness that the Lord would soon return, and this spurred them on to get things done without delay. Today, we have often little awareness of that kind, and have simply settled down comfortably.

The early Christians furnish us with the model of a church, at once familial, missionary and deeply attached to God. From them we learn the value of remaining close to Christ, and of friendship with him. The genuineness of our bond with him is shown by the love we have for each other: 'By this shall all know you are my disciples, if you have love for one another' (Jn 13:35). The young Christian community practised this so that people really did say: 'See how they love one another.'

We learn moreover from the early church to value Christian community. It was said of the first Christians that they were of one heart and soul and held everything in common. We know today that Luke was here idealising early Christian life. There were certainly conflicts and tensions in the young churches, witness Paul's letters, particularly those to the Corinthians and Galatians. Yet stronger than all conflicts was the bond of unity.

The early church provides an ideal for every Christian life, and especially for religious congregations. In various ways they have found there an impetus for their foundation. They want to model themselves on the first Christians' attachment to God, their familial bonding, their emphasis on community and missionary zeal. Like those first Christians, we too can overcome all external and internal obstacles, and press forward to the ends of the earth.

The Founder of the Society of Mary, Jean Claude Colin, sees the model of the early church mirrored in the person of Mary. She does not remain outside the church, in judgement upon it, but is a companion living among the disciples, as it were, unknown and hidden. Thus she, 'Queen of Apostles', almost disappeared in the midst of them. She was concerned not to weaken the position of Peter and the apostles, but rather to strengthen it.

Colin then projected into the future the model of the early church, with the humble Virgin Mary in its midst. That is the church as it will appear at the end of time, a church based on a person who will be invisible within it. Such a church consists of people forgetful of themselves, setting aside their own position and interests in order to serve the unity of the whole body. On that account they will foster unity with Pope and bishop, without lapsing into authoritarianism. They serve a church in which there is greater community. Mercifulness towards the needy or marginalised is always a concern for them. Contemplating Mary among the apostles, Jean Claude Colin dreams of a better church than the one today. He dreams of a church with a Marian face.

Reflection on the early church conceals within it a dynamic power. All the great reformers have taken inspiration from it. Renewal of the church has meant bringing to life again the early church. The past is often idealised in the process, and the present is criticised in the name of this idealised past, so as to open up a new future. Thus reflection on the early church conceals a lot of inflammable material regarding present day questions. It prevents the church from settling into comfortable domestication, instead of facing up to the challenges of the present and the future. The Spirit of God continually calls us to radical departures, and dispenses spiritual gifts in plenty to undertake them.

Gifts and Fruits of the Spirit
Wherever Christians get together in faith communities, in the family, parish, religious congregation or other grouping, many gifts of grace become evident. Paul names as gifts of grace: faith, knowledge, healing, prophecy, leadership and discernment of spirits. Where these gifts are translated into action, many fruits of the spirit are visible, such as love, joy, peace, patience, friendship, loyalty, gentleness (cf. Gal 5:22ff).

Those whom the church has acknowledged as saints, gave free play to the Spirit of God in their lives. On that account they were also mostly ahead of their time. So someone such as Francis of Assisi is acknowledged and treasured by both Christians and non-Christians.

Missionary thrust of the church

When the church is actively missionary, she is continually born again in various cultures. As Mary stands at the beginning of the new, the beginning of Jesus, the advent of the Son of God in this world, and also at the beginning of the church, so must the church help to instigate new beginnings.

According to the witness of Luke, the church began to grow strongly on the day of Pentecost. The first sermon of Peter struck the hearers to the heart (Acts 2:37), so that on that day three thousand people were converted (cf. Acc 2:41). Since that time the church has been implanted in the most varied cultures on earth. Christians, filled with missionary enthusiasm, have continually proclaimed the message of Christ to those who do not yet believe.

Being missionary belongs to the essence of the church. Missionary awareness is the gauge of our faith in Jesus Christ and of our love for him. The stronger and deeper the faith, all the greater will be the desire to proclaim him and to witness to him. When faith slackens, so does missionary zeal and the capacity for witness diminishes. Faith becomes strong by being passed on.

A worldwide mission has been entrusted to the church. It is her duty to proclaim the message of Jesus Christ in such a way that it can be incarnated in the various cultures. She has the task of proclaiming Christ where he is not yet known or where he is no longer known. In her missionary activity the church will look to God on the one hand and on the other to the needs of human beings. In this way the church will become receptive to God and fruitful for people.

At all times Christians have gone out into widely different parts of the world to bring the message of Christ. In the eighth century it was the Benedictines who missioned to Europe. Since the sixteenth century various missionary orders have taken part in spreading the Christian faith to other continents.

Evangelisation today: The Second Vatican Council

Through the document *Ad Gentes*, on the missionary activity of the church, the Second Vatican Council gave rise to a new awareness that mission is not only the task of some missionaries, but belongs to the essence of the church. Consequently the Council also began to make use of a new term, 'evangelisation'. It distinguished between first evangelisation and re-evangelisation. The former signifies bringing the good news of Jesus Christ to a people and a culture for the first time. Re-evangelisation means that a territory once Christian has lost its Christian roots, and must be confronted once more with the message of Christ. Often pre-evangelisation must come before such a process. It is necessary to awaken the consciousness of people to religious questions, or to make them aware of the existence of such questions.

Paul VI

Paul VI devoted his noted Encyclical, *Evangelii nuntiandi* (1975), to the theme of evangelisation. In no. 14 we read: 'Evangelising is in fact the grace and vocation proper to the church, her deepest identity. She exists in order to evangelise, that is to say in order to preach and teach, to be the channel of the gift of grace.'[4] The aim of evangelising is therefore to change people inwardly. Proclamation must take place above all through the witness of life. 'Modern man listens more willingly to witnesses than to teachers, and if he does listen to teachers, it is because they are witnesses.' Evangelisation is not, however, to be directed solely towards individuals, but also to whole cultures. 'For the church it is a question not just of preaching the gospel in ever wider geographic areas or to ever greater numbers of people, but also of affecting and as it were upsetting, through the power of the gospel, mankind's criteria of judgement, determining values, points of interest, lines of thought, sources of inspiration and models of life ...' Consequently, for Paul VI human development and liberation are closely bound up with evangelisation, even if they are not the same thing. By proclaiming the word of God in this way, we will best subscribe to building up a new society, where justice and close human relationship are better recognised.

John Paul II

In the course of his pontificate, John Paul II has extended this thinking, adding the term 'new evangelisation'.

In a period of secularisation many believers may have lost access to the word of God. So it is the task of the church to evangelise where Christ is not known, but also where Christians have lost sight of God. A second evangelisation or re-evangelisation, as John Paul writes in his mission encyclical *Redemptoris missio*, is needed in areas where whole groups of Christians have lost a living sense of faith.[5] New evangelisation is also necessary for special cultural sectors, such as foreigners, refugees, people in large towns, and for young people in general.

The Pope is convinced the new cultural environment is like the one Paul discovered in Athens, when he was preaching on the Areopagus. Evangelisation has to respect the seeds of truth in other religions, but Christ must at the same time be proclaimed with explicit conviction. Through a new evangelisation we shall contribute to 'a civilisation of love', as Pope John Paul has described it on several occasions. That would also be the best preparation for the new millennium.

Moreover, in his encyclical *Christifideles laici*, the Pope emphasises that evangelisation is above all a matter for the laity, not just for priests and religious. Such evangelisation is not only a question of words, but above all, of living witness. First of all the evangeliser must be converted. In making Christ known it is important to respect the freedom of the listeners, to win them from within their freedom.

God's word will again become incarnate in our contemporary world and history. So that we can contribute positively to this by our life and activity, it is certainly necessary to know our time and to evaluate it well. We must appreciate the wonderful scientific and technical progress achieved in the twentieth century, for example in the area of medicine or communications. On the other hand, that same century was the bloodiest in human history, with two gruesome world wars and, up to this very day, many troubled spots.

We must confront our contemporary world with God's word, so that our culture may be penetrated by the power of God's love.

4. GROWTH OF THE EVER-LIVING CHRIST

As Jesus grew up in the family community of Nazareth, and Christ grows within us spiritually after our personal conversion, so he wills also to be present within the growth of the faith community. That growth is not merely an outward increase in numbers, but still more is it inward, through every charism coming to fruition and all the fruits of the Spirit reaching maturity.

The church is of its essence more than what comes across in publicity, more than ecclesiastical hierarchy, institutions, canonical prescriptions or restrictive ordinances. The church is a spiritual entity in which Jesus Christ lives on.

When we are dealing with the growth of the church in what follows, we must not stop at the external facts, but pay attention above all to Christ living on in the church. I do not want to attempt a kind of short history of the church.[6] I simply want to point to certain stages in the history of the church in order to show clearly how it must over and over again transcend itself. The church certainly does not exist for its own sake, but to serve the kingdom of God. The more it reaches beyond itself the truer to itself the church is, because it is approaching more nearly to the kingdom of God.

Inspired by Walbert Bühlmann's vision of the church, I should like to distinguish three stages in its growth.[7]

External growth of the church

Impelled by the mighty working of the Holy Spirit, the young church spread out in explosive fashion after the Pentecost event. According to the Acts of Apostles, three thousand people were converted by the preaching of Peter (Acts 2:41). The first Christians lived together in peace and harmony (Acts 2:43-47; 4:32-37). They practised close community in prayer, mutual caring and common mission to the world. In the power of the Spirit the sick are healed (Acts 3:1-10), and the apostles preach so openly that they are soon locked up. They witness: 'It is impossible for us to remain silent over what we have heard and seen' (Acts 4:20).

But the disciples at first limit their activity to Israel, as did their Master, Jesus Christ. Jerusalem, the town in which the central saving events took place, became the first centre of their movement. They had great missionary zeal, but it was limited to Israel.

Advancing beyond the Jewish frontiers: Jerusalem – Israel
Adverse circumstances, such as persecution, were necessary in order to drive Christians away from the centre. The Spirit of God was at work in the midst of these events in such a way that the Christian body ceased to be confined to Israel. By these far reaching measures, the Spirit prevented the Christians from degenerating into a Jewish sect. The persecution was necessary in order to drive the Christians into heathen territories.

As the wind drives seeds over the countryside, so the persecution scattered the Christians over the whole of Palestine, not as lost wanderers, but as messengers and witnesses of life, as harbingers and bearers of salvation. Alight with fire from the Spirit they became bearers of that fire. Opposition and persecution do not suffice to destroy the power of life. On the contrary, this vitality grows and unfolds in the midst of threats, and indeed on account of them.

So the Spirit of God effects a broadening of their horizons through the contrary circumstances of their lives. In this way, the first non-Jew came to be baptised, the Ethiopian treasurer (cf. Acts 8:26-40).

Paul
The conversion of Paul outside Damascus was an important step. His conversion is reported three times in the Acts of Apostles: first of all Luke reports it in his own words (Acts 9:1-22), and then Paul speaks twice of his conversion to different

audiences. The second account (Acts 22:3-16) places greater emphasis on the original connection of Paul with those Jews who held strongly to the Law, whereas in the third speech (Acts 26:9-18), he makes a straightforward statement about the basic meaning and aims of the mission to the pagans. All three accounts speak of God's all-powerful intervention, striking Paul down and inwardly changing him.

The passionate persecutor of Christians will now become a tireless missionary to the pagans. Thanks to him essentially, Christianity finally stepped across the boundaries of Jewish thought and became a worldwide religion. To that end Paul did not shrink from conflict with Peter, the head of the young church. The occasion was the question as to whether those who wished to be baptised must to some extent first become Jews before they could be Christians, i.e. be circumcised and keep the Jewish laws. Paul was from the start totally convinced about the freedom of the gospel. His view was upheld by a council of the apostles. Peter, strengthened by a clear dream pointing in the same direction, could now baptise the pagan Cornelius without misgivings and anxiety.

With concentrated missionary energy, Paul journeys into Asia Minor, crosses over into Greece, gives an important speech on the Areopagus in Athens, and finally pushes right to the centre of the Roman world empire. There, in Rome, he dies a martyr's death.

The basis laid during the first phase of the church remained. The spiritual tradition has been carried on by the Eastern Church right up to our own day. It is evident in a deeply meaningful liturgy, a rich mysticism based on the resurrection, and also in a powerfully expressive iconography. The Jesus Prayer has become an especially expressive form, and is possibly even a connecting line to Buddhist thought.

Rome established centre of Christianity
Persecution in Rome
Their missionary zest drove the first apostles, Peter and Paul, to

Rome, the heart of the Empire. Of course they had to labour covertly at first, because Christianity was soon persecuted by the state. Peter and Paul both suffered martyrdom in the first persecution, under Nero. The emperor hated Christians and made scapegoats of them, accusing them of being responsible for burning down Rome. After a period of a relative quiet, persecution resumed under Trajan and Diocletian. But this could not hinder the spread of Christianity. On the contrary, the faith was strengthened. Those who were killed were honoured as martyrs.

The struggle between pagans and Christians was not carried out solely in terms of force. Many writings were directed against Christians. They were accused of being blasphemers, were deemed to be enemies of the state because they would not sacrifice to Caesar, nor honour him as a god.

Christianity, the state religion
From the beginning of the rule of the Emperor Constantine persecution ceased. Constantine ascribed his victory at the Milvian Bridge, north of Rome, to the support of the true, eternal King, Christ. He bestowed freedom on the Christian religion, and finally introduced it as the official religion of the state. Everyone must become a Christian: baptism became a condition for obtaining Roman citizenship. This law triggered off mass conversions. Rome became the centre of Christendom, and except for short intervals the Popes have resided there ever since.

Already at that time many Christians felt the danger consequent upon the elevation of Christianity to the status of official religion. The challenge of being a Christian was lost; Christianity became domesticated. Many conversions were purely external. Whenever the church becomes comfortably installed, a new Exodus is necessary. We may interpret in this way the process of radical change expected of us today.

Over long centuries there developed a close involvement of the church with political powers. In the course of the Middle Ages this led, for example, to a bitter on-going controversy between the Papacy and secular rulers, notably in Germany,

France and England, concerning their respective authority in the appointment of bishops and the financial claims of the church. Dramatic and often bloody events marked this struggle over three centuries.

Here was a rich, powerful church, a strong, efficient institution, very different indeed from the group of poor fishermen around Jesus.

A worldwide Christianity

When Columbus discovered America, and subsequently the world was circumnavigated and more continents were discovered, missionaries soon followed these discoveries, to proclaim Christianity to the people of these lands. Of course mission and colonisation often went hand in hand. The discovery and conquest of new countries went ahead with the conversion of the pagans and their incorporation into the church. Because people were convinced that every pagan was eternally lost unless baptised, some forceful means were employed to pressure people into believing. Missionary activity was widely seen to be a conquest of the hearts of people for Christ. In general, missionary activity had a European stamp.

Even then there were always missionaries against this position, who had a feeling for foreign cultures and religions. They perceived the seeds of truth there and sought to adapt themselves to other cultures, sometimes without stressing what was specifically Christian.

In any case, it is right to overcome our European orientation in order to give their due to people of other cultures. Just as Christ had become a human being, so it is valid to penetrate into other religions, not so as to adapt oneself to them, but so as to change them from within.

On the way to a world church

In our time there is an increasing awareness of the church across the world. While in the countries of the first world the church only holds its own with difficulty, in the third world it is beginning to spread vigorously. The religious orders also experience that while there is a very sparse recruitment in the first world, the number of members is increasing in third world countries. Thus Walbert Bühlmann entitles one of his books, *The coming of the third world.* The major thrust of the church is beginning to shift in that direction.

The Second Vatican Council renewed and deepened our awareness of the universal mission of the church. The church is 'Sign and instrument of union with God, and of the unity of all mankind.' These words from the introductory chapter of the *Dogmatic Constitution on the Church* are, as it were, the theme which the Council will develop. The church does not exist for its own sake, but is sacrament of the unity of all mankind. It is the task of the church to implant the faith in all cultures, as the Mission Decree says. It is necessary to develop a sensitivity to the cultures of other countries, but also to perceive their limitations. We must be aware of where the gospel is critical of a culture and of how the gospel can advance it. It is necessary to engage in a lively dialogue with the great world religions connected with other cultures. We stand here at the beginning of a vast, fascinating development.

May we, like Mary, be open to the new that God sets before us today. As Mary was open to the new in Nazareth, that is, to the coming of God into the world, and open to the new in the coming of the Holy Spirit upon the young community at prayer in the upper room, so must we too be open to the new that is emerging at this time.

Change of theological perspective
Theological development involves constantly progressing beyond the present way of looking at things. If we now reflect on this development we shall not presume to work through an abbreviated version of two thousand years of theological history![8] We will just select certain characteristic stages, from which it can be seen how theological thought must always reach beyond itself.

From Jewish thinking to Christian consciousness
Christianity originated in a Jewish thought context, heavily imprinted by monotheism*. Jesus himself prayed in the Temple to Yahweh, using the words of the psalms, and read in the synagogue from the scriptures of the Old Testament. Likewise, Mary and the first apostles were marked with the Jewish way of thinking. But the more they entered into the thought of Jesus and understood his message of the kingdom of God, the more they were able to recognise that Jesus was far more than a Jewish prophet, that he is one with the Father in an extraordinary way.

However, from these insights to the formulation of a teaching concerning the divine sonship of Jesus Christ, and from then onward to the formulation of a Christian understanding of the Trinity was a longer way, one that led from the Council of Ephesus through the Council of Nicea to the Council of Chalcedon.

Inculturation in the Greco-Roman world
When Christianity pushed forward into the Greco-Roman cultural world, quite different questions arose. Paul gave his famous speech on the Areopagus. He spoke of walking around the town and finding an altar with the inscription 'To an Unknown God.' Taking this for a starting point he said: 'The God whom I proclaim is in fact one whom you already worship without knowing it' (Acts 17:23) From there he tries to lead on to the central message of the death and resurrection of Jesus. This speech was not crowned with success: some scoffed at him, others postponed further talk, only a few came to believe.

It was reserved for later generations to articulate Christianity by means of Greek philosophy. The philosophy of Plato* became an instrument for the theological thinking of St Augustine, and remained so in theological reflection over the next thousand years. In the thirteenth century Thomas Aquinas* developed a body of teaching making use of the philosophy of Aristotle*. This conceptual structure served theological thinking right up to our time. Thomas' *Summa Theologica* was for centuries the definitive system of theology.

The great theologians of the West, such as Anselm* of Canterbury, Bonaventure*, Thomas Aquinas were concerned to harmonise thought and faith. True faith for them is faith in the total human being. In their view, reason has an important task to fulfil within faith. It climbs up the ladder of Being, from the inorganic, through the organic up to spiritual Being, and so thrusts upwards to the highest Being, God. These theologians were still conscious that God is greater than all our thinking.

Their imitators sometimes forgot about that. God was sometimes spoken about as if he were a thing of this world. Augustine's warning, *'Quod capis, non est Deus'* ('What you grasp with your reason is not God') was forgotten. In this way they sinned against the second of the ten commandments: 'Thou shall not take the name of the Lord in vain.' One who cursed did not sin so grievously against God as one who spoke about him as though he were a mere thing of the world. This understandably evoked a philosophical critique of the proofs for the existence of God (e.g. Immanuel Kant*). The fact is, one must transcend the kind of dogmatic thinking which understands faith as a system of theories.

Transcending dogmatic thinking

We are constantly in danger of imprisoning faith in a system of beliefs and theories. But faith is always more than the sum of all known statements of faith. The more we are dealing with questions about the meaning of existence, the more those questions enter the realm of paradox. Yes, we may even say, as long as thought does not give way before the paradox of reality, it has not in fact hit upon those questions which are truly meaningful for life. Linear reasoning kills dead the whole truth of any matter, because it is stuck fast in mutually exclusive propositions. Real truth is always a drawn bow: only in that way are the harmonies of truth revealed. Kierkgaard calls paradox the real thought-form which enables us to master the future. This is specially true for the Christian message, which says it has pleased God to be victorious in the paradox of the cross.

Kierkegaard has heavily criticised theology for building magnificent cathedrals out of beautiful, spiritual thoughts, but itself dwelling in a wretched hut. Faith is more than knowing about formulas of belief. Faith is an attitude of trust in God that surrenders itself to the faith reality. Genuine faith corresponds naturally to a deep longing within people, and cannot be adopted externally. It is a matter of dwelling inside one's own theology, that is, bringing theological reflection and personal experience into a fruitful dialogue with each other.

Transcending moral consciousness

In the nineteenth century religion was understood principally as being concerned with morality. For many believers, faith consisted in carrying out fixed requirements. 'You shall', 'You must', 'You shall not'. People saw themselves as continuously exposed to demands and impositions, and they gradually began to emancipate themselves. A psychology of the person was able to demonstrate how deforming such impositions are, especially when they become internalised. At best they feed into a strong sense of religious duty, but they can also lead to an unhealthy, neurotic self-protection or compulsive scrupulosity.

For too long, faith was proclaimed in terms of religious morality instead of religious being, which extols God's grace, which is freely given but cannot be earned. The priority of being over obligation in Christ's message needs to be grasped again, and more deeply. The high demands of the Sermon on the Mount: 'If anyone hits you on the right cheek, offer him the other as well'; 'If a man takes you to law and would have your tunic, let him have your cloak as well'; 'Love your enemies and pray for those who persecute you' (Mt 5:39, 40, 44), cannot be fulfilled by one's own strength, because of the opposition put up by our emotions. We are to see in these commandments a promise of Jesus. He is saying something like: 'If you will but rely on me as the Lord of your life, you will be able to grow and mature, in such a way that in the end you will be able even to love your enemy!' He promises what people are capable of by the power of God.

Transcending metaphysical consciousness
The more human beings take on active responsibility for their lives and future, the less they are ready to pay homage to a fatalistic understanding of God. They will not expect from a transcendent God the fulfilment of their inner needs. They will no longer be put off by talk of a better future in the hereafter. They will prefer to take their destiny into their own hands.

Does such a development mean the end of the God question? Many think so. Friedrich Nietzsche saw it as a last step in surmounting consciousness of the metaphysical, which finally comes to an end with the death of the God question.

Many ideas about God have, in fact, been overtaken and are dying out. Where formerly God was claimed as the explanation for everything that happened, the wealth of possible natural explanations becomes daily more evident. A God who must serve to fill the gaps in the explanation of natural phenomena will certainly beat a continual retreat. We see more clearly now where we have projected our needs onto God, and where we have used faith as a means of being content with the promise of a better hereafter.

But does this development really mean the end of the God question? Is there perhaps even some path opening up and leading on to a deeper understanding of faith? Has some space not been made for a faith grounded in personal experience? Has the way not been cleared for a rediscovery of mysticism?

Discovering mystical consciousness
Mysticism often grows from an experience of religion lacking in spirituality, and the effort to remedy this. It grows out of experiencing the uncertainty of the wrong way. Discontent with the trivialising of faith, evident in formalised ritual, dogmatism and moralising, drives people to go more deeply into the underlying ground of faith. Ritual, doctrine and law were certainly formulated by the believing community, as expressions of God's original claim upon them, but through exaggeration of outward forms faith was alienated. Instead of the original contact with God, a

huge pile of behavioural rules and wordy expressions of the truths of faith has often been pedalled around. Discontent with institutionalisation is frequently how a longing to respond to God's primary claim is expressed. Recognition of this yearning can set us off again on our way to God, and once that hunger for him has been aroused, an endless unfolding is possible. Teilhard de Chardin voices the hope this 'will lead to a mystical responsiveness and penetrability in people'. From the all-connecting middle point of the world, Point Omega, from the cosmic Christ, a radiance goes out to all, which until now only those people experienced who were especially caught up by God. Now the time has come, however, when the capacity to respond will embrace the whole of humanity, because they cannot live any more without it.

In the midst of our God-forlorn epoch we can find our way to the God who has to do with the depth of our existence. The suffering which results from our continually unfulfilled human yearning will prove to be God's charming way of reminding us we have forgotten him! As the thought of his father's house touches the heart of the starving son and prompts him to return, so can the emptiness of people today help them find their way to God.

Inner growth of the church

Inner growth is signified where the church understands itself as 'Body of Christ' (1 Cor 12), 'Community of the Holy Spirit' (2 Cor 13:13) or 'Temple of the Holy Spirit' (1 Cor 6:19; Eph 2:21).

The church is essentially more than its visible, public appearance, more than ecclesiastical hierarchy or mere institution. The church is much more: it is a spiritual entity, in which Christ continues to live. Jesus promised his disciples: 'Where two or three of you are gathered in my name, there am I in the midst of you' (Mt 18:20). The Risen One renewed this promise in the words: 'I am with you all days, even to the end of the world' (Mt 28:20).

The inner growth of the church begins by people building up a personal relationship with Christ and living from it. It shows when a sense of community grows. In the sacraments, believers grow in their faith life and the church grows as a whole. The inner growth of the church becomes evident through the fruits of faith in everyday life, in marriage, family, occupation, etc. The church grows inwardly if it is open to those who are not yet believers, or can't believe anymore.

Growth of the church as the living Christ

The church is called to grow more and more into the attitude of Christ, who harboured an intense relation with God as his father, a deep love for us, and who realised he was sent out into the world.

Thus the interior growth of the community of believers is evidenced by its relationship with God, by relations with each other and by a deepening of apostolic mission. This inner growth of the church is shown by the liturgy, the up-building of community, and service of each other being essential components of church activity, and all three areas being as important as each other.

Liturgy

We Christians come together in the liturgy in order to praise God, to listen to his word together and to be nourished with the bread of life. We can then go out again into the world as a missioned people. Through the liturgy our bond with Christ, as head of the church, and with each other is strengthened. Church is not experienced any more just as an institution, but as a living event.

Service

What is grounded in the liturgy must develop in our daily connectedness with each other. The result of our close relationship with God is shown in how we treat each other as brothers and sisters. It shows in the way married couples treat each other, how they mutually respect one another and care for their children. It shows in how we do our job. When we live from our closeness to God, we will also concern ourselves for people in need, the sick, the unemployed, the refugees. Church grows where there is an open heart for those in any kind of need, for the hungry, thirsty, or other material want. At the core of all these needs Christ is to be found. The church grows by our accompanying and strengthening our brothers and sisters in faith on their way, and by our helping to meet the need of our time for God. By our activity in the course of everyday life, we build up community in faith.

Mission

The church will not simply restrict itself to fellow believers. When in loving openness and ready service, it turns to those who do not yet belong to the company of believers, or who have lost their way, the church is able to grow beyond its limits. It grows interiorly by opening up to the Lord, who in many different ways is advancing towards us from the future.

Relationship with God and with each other, attending together to apostolic mission are equally important. Edith Stein has expressed that strikingly: 'The more people are drawn into God, the more they must also become out-going, i.e. go out into the world to bring the divine life there.' Intimacy with God is also the best source of apostolic fruitfulness. A truly missionary spirit needs to feel at home in God.

In the various religious congregations, relationship with God, community life and apostolic mission are always viewed as essential, although with varied emphases. When either prayer or community life or mission was neglected in a spiritual group, it began to disintegrate. The group either became introverted, or dissipated in excessive action.

So a community is fruitful when it views all these elements as equally important. An interior bond with God enables the order to go out into the world with missionary zeal. It was said about Francis, often underway as a wandering preacher in the vicinity of Assisi: 'His feet could walk among the people because his heart was at home in God.' When new continents were discovered, congregations soon began to thrust outwards bringing the gospel to the new world.

To be able to meet the challenge of the new evangelising required by our time, we need to be newly and deeply anchored in God. We must nourish ourselves again from the sacraments in order to be enabled for our mission in the world today.

Growth of the church through the sacraments

In a general sense the church itself is a sacrament, that is to say, a 'sign and instrument of interior union with God and of the unity of all humankind' (*LG* 1), as the Council's document on the church succinctly puts it. The church is a sign of salvation by its proclamation of Christ, and in particular by its celebration of the sacraments. The faith community grows through this activity.

In baptism the church renews itself physically, so to speak, ensures its continuance into the next generation, and constantly reproduces a community of the reborn. Confirmation makes the community of believers a missionary church, called to carry out Christ's saving work in the here and now. In confirmation, through the charisms of each member, the church as a whole is filled with the manifold saving dynamism of Christ. In that way the church survives all tests and crises, and reaches maturity.

In the eucharist the church gathers repeatedly as the community of Christ's faithful to hear together the word of God, and to be nourished by the bread of life. Through this most splendid and powerful event that is eucharist, the church matures. By receiving the Body of Christ over and over under the form of bread, the faithful themselves become more and more the Body of Christ, that is, the church.

On its pilgrim way, the church needs to be repeatedly converted and do penance. In the sacrament of reconciliation it purifies itself of its waste and spoil, and of the scourge of recurring sin. In the sacrament of anointing the sick, the church carries out again Jesus' saving action towards its sick and infirm members.

In the sacrament of marriage the church is established in miniature. Two people, promising fidelity to each other, become the model of God's covenant with his people. The couple is enabled to live together in life-long loyalty and to be co-creators with God in the world. In the sacrament of ordination the church continuously passes to some members of the Christian body the task of proclaiming the word of God, dispensing the sacraments, accompanying fellow Christians on their way through life. The Christian community is thus built up around Christ its head.

If we constantly nourish ourselves with the sacraments, then we too will be able to deploy all the strengths given us for the up-building of the Body of Christ.

Growth and charisms

The inner growth of the church becomes evident wherever she understands herself as the Body of Christ, with him as head and the individual Christians as members. This reality was borne in on Paul at his conversion as he was approaching Damascus. Through the voice from heaven: 'Saul, Saul, why are you persecuting me?' (Acts 9:4), the identification of Jesus with his followers became clear to him. By persecuting Christians he was persecuting Christ himself. In his theology of the mystical Body of Christ and of the community of the Spirit he expresses this realisation.

The interior growth of the church appears where she understands herself as a community of the Spirit in which everyone has his or her gifts of grace for the benefit of all. Natural talents become charisms if they are deployed for all the members of the church, and not just for personal use. The various charisms are special manifestations of the Holy Spirit, given to individuals for the good of all and especially for the spread of the church.

For Paul, such charisms are the gift of wisdom, knowledge, powers of faith and healing, discernment of spirits, and many others. These gifts serve to build up, counsel and console the community.

Leadership tasks: new understanding

Whoever has to exercise leadership in the church must make sure to be aware of the gifts of the Spirit present in the faith community, and to stimulate their development and deployment. Leaders have to carry out their task in the spirit of service, with great respect for the value of the human person. They will endeavour to build up a familial community in Christ, where God is sought and loved before all else. They must be people of faith, attentive to God's word, but also able to discern the signs of the times. They must walk closely with God, and develop their own pastoral zeal while challenging others to do likewise. Where, on the other hand, leaders suppress the charisms of others or only allow scope for their own, the faith community comes to a standstill.

We are experiencing today a change in our understanding of leadership, from a commanding, directive, militaristic exercise of authority to one that seeks to challenge and stimulate. Much of the opposition to authority arises from continuing to impose the control model. A good leader pays attention to the views of the members of the group, and helps them to carry out the mission that Christ has entrusted to them. He promotes co-responsibility and carries out his charge in a collegial spirit. He constantly reminds the community of the mission entrusted to them. He is at the same time not afraid of admonishing and correcting if the mission is endangered. He will never forget that Jesus is the real head of the church. He will place Christ at the centre of his own life and help other Christians to find their way to him.

When a Christian community lives together in that attitude, the original power of Christian love comes to fruition and holds everything together. The gift of love is more important than any other. If a person should possess the gift of prophecy and know all mysteries, if one should have faith to move mountains and have not love, it would be useless. Love is patient, kind. It does not boast, nor is it proud. It does not seek its own advantage. It never gives up (cf. 1 Cor 13). Together with love come all the other fruits of the Spirit: 'Love, joy, peace, endurance, friendliness, kindness, loyalty, gentleness and self control' (Gal 5:22). Paul places these fruits of the Spirit in contrast to the many evils which proceed from the spirit of the world. He is convinced the power of love and the Spirit of God is finally stronger than evil. In the power of love the Christian community makes its way into the future.

Practice of discernment in a faith community
All these charisms, particularly the charism of love, work together to enable the community of believers to come to their decisions in faith. When all participants in the process are attentive to the guidance of the Spirit, he will show the community the will of God for the next step it must take. The process demonstrates how leadership on a spiritual basis is possible, as we shall see more fully in what follows.

To make a good decision in faith, an intensive spiritual preparation is indispensable. People must come to the process with inner openness and availability. They must from the very beginning be ready to go along with what the group will discern, even if it is contrary to their original opinion. Without this commitment to letting go, the participants cannot get involved in a common search and inquiry. Another pre-requisite is basic agreement on what is essential and important for the community. Members of a religious congregation need to be inwardly connected with their order, to be in overall agreement with its spiritual and apostolic aims, and convinced that spiritual and apostolic progress can be made through the group.

For the discernment process to succeed it is important that the problem be clearly stated, and adequate information on possible solutions be provided. If the alternatives have been clearly stated the immediate preparation of the decision process begins.

Each participant reflects prayerfully on the given alternatives. Each one endeavours to be free of personal interests, wishes and anxieties, and to come to a personal judgement, keeping in mind the common basis.

In a first round of conversation, each participant sets out his or her view simply and clearly, while the others try to give an empathetic hearing, without comment, to this statement. No discussion takes place.

Only now does the real process of deciding begin. In a first round, each person in turn sets out arguments for one solution, and in another session arguments for the other solutions. Everyone contributes all the arguments he or she can find for the alternative solutions. Pro and contra arguments from all participants are given equal attention. Between sessions there is always foreseen a time for prayer, in which each one listens to what God wants to say to him or to her, through the group.

In listening together to what each has said, a group awareness emerges that eventually makes a common faith decision possible. During the community process, the group goes through various phases: phases of agreement and disagreement, muddle and clarity, tension and whatever. If the group pays attention to these it will be enabled to make a discernment of spirits. From the Spirit of God come the stirrings that lead to faith, that arouse a creativity corresponding to the gospel and lead the community to a new joy. At the end of the process of making a decision there is understandably a readiness to undertake what has been decided together. In this way the common search for God's will and the common listening to each other reaches its objective. Each individual is then ready to carry through, in simple service, what the community has recognised as the will of God.

Simplicity in service – source of apostolic fruitfulness

At a time when people are jealous of their freedom and personal independence, a simple demeanour is specially important if we are to be effective apostles. The epoch when the church could present itself vested in power and external glory is definitively at an end. The church is called to serve in love, 'Love is never boastful or conceited ; it is never jealous' (1 Cor 13:4f).

Here Mary, handmaid of the Lord, is truly an image of the church. Despite being highly chosen, she remained one who served in simplicity. So too must we: 'In spite of the greatness of her mission and the reality of her holiness, an authentic church is where lowliness is treasured.'[9] A holy, faithful church 'does not seek to excite notice, or to disassociate itself from people, distinguish itself from them. It lives among them, shares their conditions.' It lives its holiness and fidelity amidst the daily life of people.

As Mary stepped back while Jesus went about his saving work, although she had played such a decisive role in it, so must a Christian labour simply and unpretentiously, yet effectively, and leave the outcome to God.

Simplicity opens the hearts of people to God far more than domination. Quiet service is the most effectual. When the church is true to itself, it loves to dwell in a simple house in an unpretentious place. Ecclesiastical power only serves to hide the power of God, which belongs to him alone.

The desire for freedom, personal independence, that people have today, also requires that we avoid every appearance of manipulation in matters of faith. We help others best by keeping a discreet profile in a discussion, not serving up ready-made answers, but simply listening in such a way that others can express themselves.

In advancing the gospel we behave most effectively if we try, as far as possible, to overcome authoritarian attitudes and to allow open communication to emerge.

In pastoral work a priest is most effectual if he does not want to do everything himself, but consciously hands over co-responsibility to the laity in the parish.

A missionary will work most fruitfully if he does not try to import our western style of Christianity into the mission country, but is a listener, one ready to receive, and tries to translate Christianity into the culture of the country.

If we keep in mind the hidden God, we shall be helped to bring about those changes which are required today, and to integrate them in a positive manner into our lives as individuals and communities of faith.

5. SUFFERING: PROCESSES OF TRANSFORMATION
IN THE CHURCH

Mary had to live through the suffering and death of Jesus, and many spiritual people have had to pass through the Dark Night on their way to God. In our time, the church must also undergo a similar Dark Night.

Way of change, according to John of the Cross

The way that the church must traverse in our time of secularisation, can best be described with John of the Cross as a passage through the Dark Night of Faith. That is true for the church as a whole in our western world, as also for every local church and family, for parishes and religious congregations.

We shall be helpful to others as a community of faith to the extent that we allow ourselves to enter upon the necessary way of purification. The church will also be able to offer support to all humanity, enduring the Dark Night of our time and history.

As we reflect on the suffering of Jesus, the process of secularisation can be seen to have positive features. Our age is one of darkness concerning God, but he has permitted that as a purifying experience. Nothing else remains for us to do than to undergo this exactly as Jesus underwent the night of death. Since he died for us, every night is a holy night, because it is illumined by the light of Christ. All depends on following him with the eyes of faith and opening our hearts to his God-willed purification.

Starting point: bewilderment and false directions

Beginning with the spiritual experience of the church in our time, we have lived through a series of apparently negative events. We have lived through an erosion of faith, decline in church attendance, decreased readiness to accept religious teaching and to rely on the norms set out by the church. There are fewer vocations to the priesthood and religious orders.

We experience within the church many evident shortcomings. The church harbours a wonderful treasure, the good news of the hope for which our time is crying out, but which is so often lacking. Instead of proclaiming the message of hope, however, the church often limits itself to conveying a doctrinal system. As well as that, it proceeds to raise a whole forest of commands and prohibitions. Legal prescriptions and institutions get the upper hand over the personal approach.

Just as the individual often tries to reach happiness in the wrong way, and gets stuck down a blind alley, so is it with the church in the modern world. The more it sets up rules and regulations, the less notice is taken of them. The more it emphasises its authority, the more it only succeeds in diminishing it. Are we not trying to preserve the Middle Ages in modern times? Impossible. In so far as we persist in being out of tune with our times and with the Lord, thus far will we remain bewildered and on a false track. God is expecting us to face up to this darkening of the question of his very existence, in order to lead us on further. The way through the darkness of faith is an offer of divine therapy with which we, as church, can give God-willed answers to the problems of our time.

Breakthrough at the Second Vatican Council – Release from fixations
Was not Vatican II an Exodus experience *par excellence*, when after a long period of self-imposed exile we opened up to the world? Certainly in the church it was the greatest breakthrough of the twentieth century. The Council was the most inspiring event in modern church history, through which the presence of the church to the movement of contemporary culture and spirituality was to be attained.

The church was understood as 'God's pilgrim people', which has not yet reached its goal, is still underway and therefore capable of change and in need of renewal. The laity are fully responsible members of the church. They participate in the universal priesthood, and exercise their apostolate everywhere in the world. The priest is servant of the people, not ruler. Moreover the hierarchy does not understand itself as dominating, but as serving. Co-responsibility is to be practised at every level. For this reason, certain advisory groups and councils were introduced.

The Christian churches and ecclesial communities outside the Catholic Church were recognised. Ecumenism was viewed positively and was definitely to be promoted. God's working was also seen in the non-Christian religions, and therefore they were to be understood and highly respected. The possibility of salvation is foreseen too for non-Christians and even for atheists.

The church recognises the progress of humankind, even if it cannot overlook dangers which are also present. So it sees itself as being in solidarity with the world and as serving all people, not only its own members. There is especially an explicit call for care for the weak and the poor. Growing together as a family of peoples is to be advanced by all means. Thus the Second Vatican Council grasped the questions of the time with confidence and hope, and trusting in the Spirit of God, opened ways to the future.

Farewell to ancient privilege

The price of these hopeful departures was at the same time a farewell to vested privilege. Christians experienced the aftermath of the Vatican Council in the way John of the Cross described the active Night of the Senses for the individual. Priests and religious felt challenged to leave behind hundreds of years of privilege: status, power, social prestige and religious superiority. They had to learn not to consider themselves any longer as specialists in holiness, but to walk on the way of faith together with all other believers. On the other hand, lay people had to learn to step out of their passivity, and to take on active responsibility in the church. This was a great reversal: for hundreds of years the laity had been educated to be passive.

Various fixed ideas about definite roles in the church had resulted in crippling the faith community. We recall how John of the Cross illustrated this handicap for the individual. He used the image of a bird that cannot fly as long as it is tethered, whether the line holding it back be thick or thin. Many such inhibiting bonds developed over the centuries: certain fixed religious ideas, forms of devotion and prayer. Vatican II now called upon us Christians to break out of these. Many were delighted

to do so and ready to leave behind narrow, restricting situations.
Others felt more anxious about the consequences.

Happy phase
John of the Cross had described the exodus, leaving the old
thing behind, getting past the immediate obstacle, as first of all a
happy experience of liberation from restrictions. Was not the
first period after the Council characterised by just such euphoria?
No task was too heavy, no risk too great, no meeting too long to
respond to our role in God's People. We developed new forms
of prayer, of ecumenical dialogue, began to make personal re-
treats, invest a lot of time in building up a new style of community, interest ourselves more in the rights of the oppressed and
in world peace. Like those whom John of the Cross calls begin-
ners, we now thought we had reached the goal of an all embracing renewal. John warned people in this situation against spiritual pride and false security.

Path through the wilderness – Liberation and change
The individual Christian has to endure a period of deep purification after a time of euphoria; likewise the church has also to
submit to passive cleansing, while God himself clears away the
deep roots of ill health.

We have noted above that, as a result of secularisation, we
are experiencing today a painful disintegration at many levels of
church life, but also the slow destruction of fixed ideas in the
area of ritual, doctrine and law. The church often tries to counter-
act this in every possible way. Counter-strategies are being
deployed with much effort and often with little effect, to halt or
at least to delay disintegration. The process simply cannot be
halted. Nothing can be done, except by …

Addressing the problem in a positive manner
Of course the church must work against the dissolution of the
inalienable core of the Christian message. It is, however, more
than ever necessary to grasp that much of what appears to be

disintegration in the realm of ritual, dogma and morality, is a dissolution of what has become alien or petrified. We must overcome the danger of locking up the Spirit of God in our own protective thinking, and in our institutions.

More than formerly, it matters to discover the personal way of faith of the individual, and without neglecting the aspect of community, to take seriously how God approaches him or her directly.

All those who exercise leadership in the church today are strongly challenged to understand their office as a service. The laity are challenged as Christians to take on active co-responsibility. The path leads from the Christian community that is looked after to the one that does the looking after.

In the future we shall perhaps be numerically smaller, but if we live our Christianity with conviction we can do great things. Another way of looking at the church quietly emerging, is that it has discovered the mystical dimension of faith. Where once there was too much outward leadership, we shall now be urged towards inner leadership. Where there was too much law, we are now challenged to emphasise mercy.

Thus we shall find our way to an unobtrusive presence of the church, a hidden and unknown ... but exceedingly fruitful ... presence in the world today. We are challenged to recognise the due place of the laity in the church. We have to look courageously at our situation and mobilise the spiritual power of faith and hope.

Temptations

Certainly the way through the Dark Night is dangerous and many people avoid it. Two temptations lie on the way. The first consists of trying to return to earlier forms of devotion, that is, to be conservatives, even fundamentalists. The other temptation is to surrender too easily. The reason why many priests and religious in recent years have given up their call is surely that they found no meaning in the Dark Night of their spiritual life.

Experience of Chaos

The way through the Dark Night is for the church, no doubt, an experience of chaos. Let us not forget, however, that chaos bears within itself the potential to be faced with the creative power of God. Chaos, bewilderment, darkness can, through that creative power, by his mercy, lead to a powerful new life if we allow it do so.[10]

This creative power led the Israelites in darkness during the exodus from Egypt. Later they must wander through the wilderness without understanding why. Their way led through spiritual darkness, so that they began to murmur against Moses. On their entry into the Promised Land, this dark phase only temporarily ended. The prophets must again call the people of Israel and their leaders to repentance. They took part in the disintegration of their people during the imprisonment at Babylon and promised that God would make a new covenant with his people.

Night and salvation history

As church we commemorate various nights in the history of salvation, nights in which God's dealings are evident. The liberation of the Jews from imprisonment in Egypt began in the middle of the night. The Jews have kept this in mind at all periods by celebrating the Paschal meal at night.

Jesus was born during the night in a stable at Bethlehem. He often prayed to his Father during the night. In the night before his passion he wrestled with his Father's will on the Mount of Olives. He was taken prisoner and judged during the night. According to the evangelists, when Jesus was dying the whole cosmos was wrapped in darkness. At night, the most precious night in world history, Christ rose from the dead. As Christians we celebrate the 'Holy Night' (*Weihnachten*/Christmas) and Easter night. From then the church has recognised the practice of prayer during the night, and keeps vigil at the great festivals. May reflection on the holy nights of salvation help us to pull through the night of God's darkness that we must endure at this time.

Let us pray to the Holy Spirit who was mightily at work at
the founding of the church, that he may help us now, as church,
to undergo in a positive way, those processes of change he expects
of us.

Holy Spirit, come to us,
sunder the darkness of our night.
Come, shine light into this world …
When we are restless you grant us quiet,
You breathe coolness on us in the heat.
Without your animating breath
Nothing can endure in us.
Wash away our stains,
Wash us clean.
On our dryness pour your dew.
Heal our wounds, life renew.
Loose the stiff, the paralysed.
Warm the numb, the chilled.
Guide our steps from wandering on the way.

This prayer speaks of many unhealthy situations in our life:
darkness, hardness, sickness, coldness, paralysis and ossific-
ation. At the same time it expresses the conviction that the Spirit
of God is a match for the demon in our time and in ourselves,
and will prove the stronger. As we said, since Christ has passed
through the Dark Night of death, every night is a holy night,
illumined by the Light of Christ.

A process of collective death
The change required of us is to accept the passing away of an
older form of church, a process of dying that has phases not
unlike those of human physical death. The church also goes
through a phase of denial, when Christians, like the individual
faced with death, sweep away the notion that there is any need
for change. There is a phase of anger, when Christian people
hang on to old traditions, defending them against any change.
Then there is a phase of bargaining, when changes are slowly
admitted, provided we can dictate how they will be.

There follows a phase of depression: with a resigned attitude, Christians let change happen, but refuse to take any hand or part in it. Finally, at the end of this process we hopefully reach the point of agreement, where we actively accept the necessary changes, even plan and further them so that they can happen in a constructive way.[11]

The church as helper in our time of change
If we are ready as church to go through the Dark Night of faith, we can also help other people to find the way through that darkness.

Modern culture in radical change
Our modern culture is undergoing a radical change. On the one hand our age has brought about wonderful technical advances. By means of modern rocketry humans have thrust out into space and landed on the moon. Medicine has been able to overcome many diseases and life threatening illnesses. Computer technology will enable humankind to make an as yet unforeseeable outreach in research. In certain respects humans have wrested for themselves various attributes of God: omniscience (via the media), omnipresence (via air and space travel) and omnipotence (atomic energy). Of course these are only limited, artificial reproductions of the divine attributes. All too often these powers slip out of human control. Thus our last century was also the bloodiest in history. Never have there been so many and such extensive wars, in which countless millions were killed. Today, through atomic energy we have the fearful ability to destroy the whole human race. This became evident at the end of the World War II, with the dropping of atom bombs on Hiroshima and Nagasaki. Since then these destructive capabilities have greatly increased, but thank God there has also been an increasing realisation: 'Never again!'

Moreover, we are able as never before to exploit the raw material of our earth, pollute the environment and destroy the basis of our own life. In this situation we are urgently called upon to change. According to Enomiya Lasalle* mankind stands before a turning point such as only occurs once in centuries.[12]

God and suffering

Following on the terrible experiences of the two world wars, authors such as Bert Brecht*, Wolfgang Borchert* and Günther Grass* directed very critical questions to God, as to why he allows mankind to take such tortuous paths, and whether he has any interest in us at all.

Borchert in his play, *Draußen vor der Tür*, has Bechmann, a returned soldier, quarrelling with the old man who represents God. 'Why do they call you "our dear Lord"? Are you really "dear", my "dear God"? Were you that "dear" when my little boy, only a year old, when you let my little boy be blown to bits by a screaming bomb? Were you "dear" when you let him be murdered, "dear God"? Where were you then when the bombs screamed down, "dear" God? Were you "dear" in Stalingrad, "dear God", were you "dear" there? When were you really "dear", "dear God", when? When have you ever bothered about us? ... We looked for you, God, in every shell-crater, every night. We called on you, God. We screamed for you God, wept and cursed! Have you turned away from us? Have you walled yourself up in your fine old churches, God? Do you not hear our cry through the rattling windows, God? Where are you?'

For generations people faced with suffering have hurled their 'Why?' against God. Confronted by the frightful experiences of the second world war, this question has acquired a special urgency. For Jews there is in addition the question of why God permitted millions of them to be killed in a gruesome, inhumane manner in the concentration camps. Auschwitz has become a byword for unspeakable cruelty. How can anyone believe in God after Auschwitz? Has Auschwitz not changed the question of God? Have words such as 'almighty', 'kindly' not dropped out of the image of God? Have we not experienced, in a dramatic fashion, the concealment and darkness of God?

Thus the dreadful events of two world wars pose for people

today very critical questions about God, his might, his sense of justice, his interest in humankind. If we do not avoid these questions, we shall soon discover ourselves asking very critical questions about ourselves too. If we want to survive, we will only be able to deal constructively with the ever growing possibilities of new technology by deepening our relationship with God. How can we grow as humans in such a way that we no longer solve conflicts by making war? How can we find new ways to peace and reconciliation?

On the road to a new consciousness
By using atomic power we can destroy the whole of humanity. If we want to survive, then our ethical sense of responsibility must grow to keep pace with technical development.

Is all humankind not developing from childhood to adulthood? Do not the insights concerning the spiritual development of individuals and of the believing community, also apply to the whole of humanity? Are we not witnesses of how humanity is going through a difficult process of restructuring?

Jean Gebser* thinks humanity has now gone the full way from archaic to rational consciousness, by way of the magical and mythical. Until today, humankind has been strongly marked by rationality. The limitations of this way of knowing are increasingly evident. The constraints of rational understanding only allow us to grasp a small part of reality. The rest escapes us. Above all, conceptual thinking does not suffice to enable us to grasp divine reality. Enomiya Lasalle believes humankind cannot get any further without arriving at another level of consciousness, which may be called integral, or wholistic. In this new form of consciousness the old will be surpassed rather than eliminated. He believes this process is furthest advanced in Europe, because there the problems arising from extant thinking stand out in sharpest relief. People have gradually become ripe for these new forms of thought. However, on the road to this new consciousness lie many problems and difficulties. Many who are at home in rational thinking, show recent signs of existential angst.* No doubt a hard time lies before the break through to another form of awareness. Only if we allow ourselves as human beings to undergo this radical change will we find our way into the future. (cf. *Digression: Towards a New Humanity*)

Yearning for fuller life

In this time of radical change we come across many people with hungry hearts. In this we are similar to the many people whose hungry hearts drove them to Jesus. Such were the tax-collector Zachaeus or the rich young man, the woman by Jacob's Well, the woman who was a public sinner, and many others.

In like manner, the longing for a happy life awakes in many people today, even if that yearning has been covered up by external preoccupations, such as drive for success, noise and activity. In us humans there is a thirst that God alone can satisfy. Human emptiness brings the fullness of God into play. 'God cannot leave anything empty and unfulfilled. The God of creation cannot endure anything remaining empty and unfulfilled … If there be anything empty under heaven, whatever it be, great or small, heaven will either draw it up to itself, or bow down to it and fill it with itself.' For Meister Eckhart it is like a natural law that a void draws God to itself. The emptiness of the human being works on God like suction. The created abyss calls to the uncreated abyss of God.

May we be alert as church, so that we can enter into the deeper longings of people today. May we be alert, so that their experience of insufficiency may become a gateway to grace. It is precisely our time of darkness concerning God that calls out for God to come. 'What is this darkness? What is its name?' asks Meister Eckhart, and he answers: 'It is nothing other than the possibility of receiving, the predisposition to receive, that which will fulfil you.' 'Whenever God finds you ready he must act, and pour himself into you.'

In the darkness of our time, may we be able like Mary to hold ourselves ready for the working of God. May we learn from Mary to cope with the radical changes of the time in an attitude of faith, of openness to the leading of God's Spirit. In her readiness to receive the Holy Spirit and to become mother of Jesus she had to play a very active role. Often she did not understand God, but she kept everything in her heart. From Mary we can learn to cope with the process of radical change which besets us today.

If we as church make our own the joys and hopes, cares and anxieties of people today, if we also proclaim the good news of the redemption, we shall be able – although only a little flock – to make a worthwhile contribution to dealing with the specific problems of our time (*Gaudium et Spes*,1). If in the midst of the needs of our age we give fearless witness to our faith and hope, we shall reach more people beyond the church buildings than if we could look out over full congregations in huge churches, as once we used to.

6. NEW MISSION: MARIAN FACE OF THE CHURCH

The divine mission that falls to us as church is continually renewed. Today we are called upon to realise some of the as yet unrealised possibilities of church.

At a time of secularisation we are challenged to advance beyond the sphere of our own church, to enter into a dialogue with all other Christian confessions, and indeed with all who believe in God in the various world religions. The declarations of Vatican II concerning the various ways in which the confessions and religions are directed towards Christ, opens the door to new and unlimited developments. The Council voiced its appreciation of what God works through other religions. In this area we are really at a beginning and eagerly anticipating the truths God has to open up to us still further.

As well as its being the community of all believers, the Council also emphasised the pilgrim nature of the People of God. The privileged position of priests and religious is no longer stressed, but the fact of being on the way together. Leadership is understood as service, not as superiority. Accordingly the mission of the laity, proceeding as it does from baptism and confirmation, is newly understood. A mighty theme, still to be dealt with, is the position of women in the church.

As church we, like Mary, are always beginning again. We are called to do great things with small means. It is important, then, to trust in God, to be hopeful and to be open to the future.

Hope and orientation to the future
Perseverance in blessed hope characterised the basic stance of the early Christians. In worldly terms they had little enough to gain. Their sights were directed at 'the appearing of the glory of our great God and saviour Christ Jesus' (Tit 2:13). Their calls sounded in the night: 'Maranatha – Come, Lord Jesus, come soon' (cf. Rev 22:20).

Today, at a time of transition and new beginnings, it is so important to be hopeful. Mary is here a model. She has arrived; we are still underway. She is 'Sign of sure hope and comfort to God's pilgrim people'(*LG*, 68). 'All Christian believers should constantly beseech the Mother of God and our Mother, that she who supported the church at its beginning, may intercede for us in heaven, until all the families of the peoples are gathered in peace and harmony into a single People of God' (*LG*, 69).

Marian face of the church
A church with a Marian face is essentially one that is coming into being and growing. On every level it is set for growth: in union with God, in awareness of community and of mission.

Growth in union with God – mystical church
A church with a Marian face will endeavour to grow ever more deeply into Christ. It will help individual Christians to advance in personal depth to a truly mystical union with God. It will have a feeling for the divine mystery lying deep in everyone's soul. It will also be conscious that as a community of believers it is a mystical entity, the Body of Christ, the living Christ. In a church thus understood, all institutions, canonical prescriptions, ethical norms, and official teachings are at the service of a spiritual reality.

A church with a Marian face is open to the emerging future.

It counts always on the greater possibilities of God. Like Mary, the church gives consent, because with God nothing is impossible.

Growth in community awareness – familial church
A church with a Marian face is aware of the communitarian nature of faith. By hearing the word of God together and following it we become brothers, sisters, mothers. We understand that we are the pilgrim folk of God. We do not reject hierarchy and office, but they are completely at service for building up the community. We know we are called together to holiness and to witness for Christ.

Mary prayed together with the apostles for the coming of the Holy Spirit, and so a church with a Marian face will continuously deepen the community element of its faith. It will avoid as far as possible every polarisation into right and left, conservative and progressive. It will carry the tension that exists between the institutional church, theological research, mission and the dream of a church of love. It will recognise the legitimate place of all these dimensions and promote a fruitful dialogue between them. It will endeavour to overcome the distrust between a Pauline, Petrine or Johannine church and to foregather all around one Lord.

Growth in openness to the whole world – a missionary church
A church with a Marian face is sensitive to the needs of our time. 'The joy and hope, sorrow and anguish of people today, especially the poor and oppressed of all kinds, are also the joy and hope, sorrow and anguish of the disciples of Christ.' This statement at the beginning of the Pastoral Constitution *Gaudium et Spes,* is as it were, the theme description of the place of the church in our world today. A church with a Marian face will be conscious of the needs of our time, and particularly of the need modern people have for God.

With all believers in all the world religions, with all people of good will, we enter into a lively dialogue with each other. What a vast, unworked field is open there! In common with all people of goodwill a church with a Marian face will stand for peace and justice among the peoples.

Growth in simplicity

A church with a Marian face is aware that we are still far from this goal, but that we are moving towards it step by step. We do not know all the answers, but we are looking for them. Consequently, we are ready to be open to the process of radical change in our life and times. We acknowledge the dark side of our life and hold it up to the Lord. We also recognise the faults of fellow human beings, but we are willing to forgive. Thus we can grow inwardly together. We are a church with a heart, a church of mercy and healing.

Case for a Marian church – Personal witness of François Marc

We should like to conclude with the personal witness of a French Marist, François Marc. He gave this impressive witness at the General Chapter of the Marist Fathers in 1993. Since then he has died, alas, at the early age of forty-seven. His witness to hope stands, nevertheless, and remains unforgettable. It fits in with what we want to say here.

The Marian church follows Mary into the mountains, going off with her to encounter life; she visits men and women, and, though things may seem to be sterile, she is on the watch for what is coming to birth, for possibilities, for the life which beats in things.

The Marian church rejoices and sings. Instead of bemoaning its fate and the world's woes, she is in wonder at the beauty there is on the earth and in the human heart, as she sees what God is doing there.

The Marian church knows that she is the object of a gratuitous love, and that God has the heart of a mother. She has seen God on the doorstep, on the lookout for the improbable return of a son; she has seen God throw his arms round the son's neck, place the festal ring on his finger, and himself organise the home-coming feast. When she pages through the family album, she sees Zacchaeus in his sycamore, the woman taken in adultery, the Samaritan woman, foreigners, the lepers, beggars and a common prisoner at his place of execution. So you see, the Marian church despairs of no one, and does not quench the smoking flax. When she sees someone on the side of the road wounded by life, she is moved by compassion, and with infinite tenderness tends their wounds. She is the safe harbour, who is always open, the refuge of sinners, *mater misericordiae*, mother of mercy.

The Marian church does not know the answers before the questions are asked. Her path is not traced out in advance. She knows doubt and unease, night and loneliness. That is the price of trust. She takes her part in the conversation, but makes no claim to know everything. She accepts that she must search.

The Marian church lives in Nazareth in silence and simplicity. She does not live in a palace. Her home is like all the other homes. She goes out to chat with the other villagers. She weeps with them, she rejoices with them, but she never preaches to them. Above all she listens.

The Marian church stands at the foot of the cross. She does not take refuge in a fortress or in a chapel or in a prudent silence when people are being crushed. She is vulnerable in her deeds and in her words. With a humble courage she stands alongside the most insignificant.

The Marian church lets in the wind of Pentecost, the wind which impels one to go out, which unties tongues. In the public square, not for the sake of hammering doctrine, nor to swell her ranks, she proclaims her message: the promise has been kept, the fight has been won and the dragon crushed forever. And this is the great secret which she can only murmur: to win the victory God has laid down his arms. True, we are in an intermediate time, the time of human history. And that history is a painful one.

Yet every evening at the end of vespers the church sings the *Magnificat*. For the church knows where her joy is to be

found. And look: God has not found our world or its afflic-
tions, its violence or its wickedness uninhabitable. It is there
that he has met us. And there, on the cross, we have seen the
'mercy', the open heart of God.

There at the foot of the cross a people was born, a Marian
people. Seeing his mother and near her the disciple whom he
loved, Jesus said to his mother: 'Woman, this is your son.'
Then to the disciple he said: 'This is your mother.' From that
moment, the disciple made a place for her in his home.

Brothers and sisters, let us belong to this people. Let us
make a place for Mary in our home. Let us enter with her into
the 'humble and heart-rending happiness' of loving and
being loved. And, in the words of Thérèse of Lisieux, the
church will be in this world, 'a heart resplendent with love'.

CHAPTER FOUR

Finding ourselves in a picture of Mary

In conclusion I should like to invite you to cast your mind back over our reflections. Rather than use words, I would prefer to call up some images of what I have been saying.

First of all, come with me and look inside the most famous Marian church in the world, St Mary Major, in Rome. The interior is essentially the same as it was when erected by Pope Sixtus III, immediately after the Council of Ephesus (431), had declared Mary to be 'Mother of God'.

This was the first Roman basilica founded by a Pope. The earlier ones were established by an Emperor, in honour of the three pillars of the church: Peter, Paul, and John. The imperial basilicas give an impression of a solid institution, and they emphasise the hierarchical aspect of the church: 'You are Peter, and upon this rock ', etc. In contrast, St Mary Major was consecrated to Mary, and later also to the founder, Sixtus, *episcopus plebi Romani,* i.e. bishop of the ordinary people of Rome.

Wherever Mary comes into the picture a new ecclesiology* is born. The church is not only seen as an institution, but above all as the People of God. Thus the basilica of St Mary Major points to an understanding of church that the Second Vatican Council has renewed. The Council prioritises what we all have in common. It emphasises that we, as church, make up together a single pilgrim people of God, and are together called to holiness. Only after confirming this priority did the Council deal with the various offices in the church, that are to minister to the well-being of the Body of Christ.

In chapter eight of the *Constitution of the Church* (*Lumen Gentium*), the Council speaks of Mary as the image of the

Church. Thus it was in keeping that Paul VI, at the end of the
Second Vatican Council, chose this church of St Mary Major in
which to celebrate Mary as 'Mother of the Church' and to proclaim the Council's vision of a church bearing the features of
Mary.

Pictures of Mary

In many Roman churches objects are venerated as relics of
Christ's life. Such devotion is a real expression of faith, even
when the genuineness of the objects themselves is extremely
doubtful!

In Mary Major many of the pictures and objects refer to
Mary. Under the high altar a shrine is shown containing what is
said to be the crib from Bethlehem. The veneration of the crib
underlines the reason for building this church, namely because
Mary gave human birth to God.

Along the walls on both sides of the nave, there is a succes-
sion of mosaics depicting scenes from the Old Testament, for
Mary's life is embedded in salvation history. These mosaics and
those on the triumphal arch date back to the foundation.

In the apse are the four principal Marian themes, to be found
in innumerable representations everywhere in the world:

Mary, the Virgin … receiving the good news from the angel;
Mary, the Mother … who has brought her son into the world;
Mary, the Woman of Sorrows … here represented by the
Flight into Egypt;
Mary, the Queen … in royal robes, being crowned — larger
than life.

The ceiling, from a much later date, and the rich gold ornament-
ation signifies not wealth but grace, and the world beyond, the
broad spaces of eternity where saints and angels meet.

These four great themes are also symbolic statements of what
I have wanted to express in this book.

The Pilgrims' Picture: Maria, salus populi Romani.

At the front of St Mary Major, on the left, there is a side chapel.

Now known as the 'Borgia Chapel', it has from the very beginning been a holy place. A picture is venerated there, an icon*
entitled *Maria, salus populi Romani*, i.e. 'Mary, salvation of the
Roman people', and no Roman visiting the church would fail to
stop before it, at least for a moment. Legend has it going back to
St Luke, and certainly the Byzantine artist who painted it, proba-
bly in the ninth century, caught the feeling of Luke in depicting
the mystery of Mary.

You can see a copy of this icon on our front cover The connection between God and humankind is illustrated here in the very
colours the artist has used. The dark garment Mary is wearing
represents the earthiness and darkness of unredeemed
mankind. The happy child she carries on her arm, dressed in
brown gold, holds a scroll which represents divine power and
knowledge breaking into the world. He sits enfolded into
Mary's dark garment, held in the earthiness of the world, with
only his head against the light. He holds out the fingers of his
right hand in a gesture signifying eternity (the circle) and his nature as God and Man (his two fingers apart). He gazes out beyond the edge of the picture into time and space.

Beneath a sparkling crown, a dark countenance looks down
at us, the face of a tall, thin, quiet woman, her serious expression
strangely moving. The woman has seen everything, nothing
unholy that people have perpetrated since the fall of Adam remains hidden from her.

This woman, holding her cheerful, friendly child, understands everything and judges nothing. She knows all the errors
and confusions the human heart can generate. She keeps silent,
her mouth firmly closed. Only her presence admonishes. The
picture is ancient, yet in some mysterious way it is almost of the
present too. Over the centuries innumerable people have come
here to pray to the understanding woman, to look at her and to
allow her to look at them.

Retrospect and Outlook
Now I would ask you also to come on pilgrimage with me to St

Mary Major's in Rome, and to look at the picture we have just been describing.

First take a little time to quieten yourself. Now run quietly over some of the thoughts in the book, what I have been saying about the life of Mary, the spiritual growth of each one, and of the community of believers.

Here we are, in the church of Santa Maria Maggiore, the most significant Marian church in the world. Here is depicted ... a church with a Marian face ... a church that does not lord it over people ... a church that knows she is a community of believers, God's pilgrim people.

Inside the building we go up to the side chapel, on the left at the front. We look intently at the pilgrims' picture, the icon, 'Mary, salvation of the Roman people'. We allow the picture work upon us. As we gaze we see ...

A woman in dark clothes, holding a joyful child on her arm. She has a serious expression. She is clothed in the colour of our earth, our darkness, but she is holding in the crook of her arm the hope of the whole world, the redeemer of humankind.

We allow our gaze to rest there on this woman ... She is familiar with the highs and lows of human life ... She knew the joy of the conception and birth of the Lord ... She accompanied him on his way ... She lived through misunderstandings and grief ... She stood by the cross ... She waited with longing for the fulfilment of the promises given by her son ... she awaited the coming of the kingdom of God ... experienced the Easter victory of her son ... She has been taken into the glory of God.

Now let her gaze rest on you ... she who knew all life's ups and downs ... let her look at you ... she who has reached the fullness of life ... let her look at you ... she who is now in glory with God, and pleads for us there ... and now, let yourself have a talk with her!

Mary, you are virgin
Yours the joy of being addressed by God himself, and conceiving Christ. Yet you also know what it is to be alone, enveloped in

your aloneness, unable to speak to anyone about what is stirring you most deeply. You know too the happiness everyone feels at being deeply understood. You can praise God for the great things he has done for you, the joy he has given you.

May we also be open to receive God, have the courage to create a quiet place within ourselves. Help us not to miss the call of God, nor to avoid him amid the noisiness of our world. Fill us with joy at the gifts your Son has given us, and enable us to respond to them thankfully.

Help us as church to be open to the call of God to us. Help us to overcome our tendency just to go along with things, the real heresy of our time, and to trust in the Holy Spirit, who is also there at work among us.

Mary, you are mother

You have brought Jesus into the world, not only your son but its Redeemer. You bore him in a stable, wrapped him up, laid him on the straw. For his sake you took on exile, and yet you continually experienced God's blessing and protection in new and surprising ways.

A loving mother, you often carried your happy child about on your arm. Over the years in Nazareth, when he was growing up, you cared for him with motherly love.

Your son, Jesus Christ, our Lord, wants to be born in us too. He wants to dwell also in the stable of our lives. May we be ready to accept him into our lives. Our interior is often just as miserable as that stable in Bethlehem. Help us to prepare a worthy dwelling for your son, who returns to us in every communion. Help us to tidy up our inner life. May we never leave your son standing outside the door, and no longer be heedless of him who meets us daily in so many ways – in the word of scripture, in people's need, in the call of the present moment.

May we allow Christ to grow to maturity within us. Help us to make the necessary room in our lives for the divine to work in us, so that we may bear rich fruit.

Help the church to proclaim the message of Christ, your son, the Redeemer of the world, convincingly and with missionary zest. Grant us the strength to proclaim Christ to people who have never heard of your son, to preach the message to those who have forgotten him, calling him again to mind.

Bless all those people who have been born again in water and in the Holy Spirit, that they may recognise their high vocation and live it. Be with all Christians so that the charisms they have received from God may be used to benefit others.

Mary, you are the woman of sorrows

You are standing by the cross. You must surrender your dear son, the very heart of your vocation, and watch him die a cruel, shameful death. You had often enough endured situations where you simply did not understand this son of yours. You had traversed many another dark place before reaching the fathomless darkness of the cross. Here, nonetheless, you receive another mission: you become mother of the disciple whom Jesus loved, and in his person, mother of all believers.

You know we pass through many dark experiences and our lives are paved with many casualties, that our faith is often dark.

Grant us the grace to let go inwardly of people and things so dear to us, and to trust that God will take us forward. Help us to be brave in facing changes the Lord is encouraging us to undertake, and to believe in the new life which will spring from them.

Intercede with your son for all who are suffering from violence and war, that they may be open to peace and reconciliation.

You know the church in our secularised world has to go through many dark experiences. Many of the trimmings accumulated over centuries are disappearing. Help the church in our day to abandon itself with confidence to the transformations expected of it, to concentrate on the essential, and to leave everything superfluous behind.

Mary, you are our Queen

You have reached the fullness of your life, you are with your beloved son. Now you are crowned in glory, our intercessor at the throne of God. You take us all under your protection, as it were beneath the shelter of your mantle.

You know that we are still wandering on earth and must still pass through all manner of darkness. With all the world's pilgrims we come to you, salvation of the people of Rome, salvation of the people of the world. We are coming with all our own cares and needs, and all those of our time. You are the sign of sure hope and confidence for the pilgrim people of God.

You have already reached the goal of all our pilgrimage. Give us courage and confidence to see the divine light behind the darkness. For all that has happened to you is also promised to us. Help us to live always in view of this fulfilment.

Help the church to be and to act more and more as you have done. May a church emerge, knowing itself to be a people on their way to God together, a simple, merciful church, a church manifestly willing and ready to serve.

We are happy, in this period since the Second Vatican Council, to live at a time when such a church is emerging. Help us to advance it still more.

We beseech you for us men and women, that we may constantly find ways to reach out to each other, ways of peace and reconciliation.

Almighty and merciful God, you have given us your son's Mother to be our mother too. Grant that we may look to this sign of hope and consolation. Grant that keeping her in view we may faithfully follow Christ, and remain on the path that leads to your glory. Amen

Towards a new humanity
Further to *On the road to a new conscious*, pp 135-36

While endeavouring to renew the face of the church, we are living in expectation of something wholly new, the one who comes. As Christians we see finally, in what is advancing towards us from the future, the returning Lord. He is heralded in what is happening and in what is important today. The human race as a whole develops from childhood to maturity as does the individual, but with this difference: the individual takes a few decades, whereas the race takes thousands of years. The human race was also conceived and born, and is destined to reach maturity.

Conception
In order to investigate human origins one would not only have to go back to the primates, but also take account of the entire evolutionary chain right back to inorganic matter. Then it would become evident that the spiritual is already present in the material and still more in the vegetable and animal sphere. It would be interesting to reflect on the development of human consciousness, to deal with the conception, birth and growth of humanity to the present day, but this would take us too far afield.[1] Let us concentrate rather on the important steps the human race must take today.

Birth of the new humankind
We are experiencing now the birth pangs of the new human being, who wants to take responsibility for shaping the world. Up until the Middle Ages people thought in collective terms. Since the Reformation and especially since the Enlightenment they began to mature as persons, conscious of making individual decisions. This is expressed in Martin Luther's statement at

the Diet of Worms: 'Here I stand. I can do naught else. God help me.' Luther felt called to remain true to his own path, even though he ran into the mass opposition of the general public and the church. Luther was not repeating simply what others had said before him. He was forming his own opinion. He was starting from 'self-confessed immaturity', as Immanuel Kant expresses it. Thus he begins to work out of principles that characterise modern people. *Sapere aude,* i.e. 'Have courage to attend to your understanding.'[2]

People are suffering from the birth pangs of a new way of thinking, just as every mother suffers while bringing her child into the world. Many hope for a return to old ways, but more thoughtful people know there is no return. The wheel of history cannot be turned back. Sooner or later the birth hour of the new humanity will arrive. We shall not be asked whether we like it or not. It will simply happen. All that matters is that the new people be strong and healthy, not still-born.

The new people are characterised by great personal freedom. They cannot forego being asked to share in making decisions about many things. This has repercussions in the religious sphere. Traditional faith does not come to many people anymore, and is becoming continually weaker. People want to have their own faith experience, and only find peace in that. The new people only come to a faith which does not depend on the belief of the environment, but is so deeply rooted in themselves that they are not shattered by unbelief in their surroundings.

The new thinking is characterised by ability to experience God in the now and to discover the hidden God in our times. The new thinking must be deeply anchored in God, a thinking that has undergone long purification.

Increasingly we come up against the limitations of our present rational thinking. There are whole areas of reality it does not cope with. Awareness of the insufficiency of present thinking is especially marked in the western world and is a symptom of the intellectual change in the offing.

Radical change – Transformation

In many respects a radical change in the exact natural sciences has become evident since the beginning of the twentieth century. For instance, in the outstripping of euclidean geometry by the idea of a four dimensional space-time continuum, in the development of quantum physics (Max Planck) and the theory of relativity (Albert Einstein). In the field of biology this change is expressed in the theory of evolution, in psychology especially in the penetration of the unconscious (Freud, Jung), and in philosophy it is seen in the eclipse of the *philosophia perennis** of a Thomas Aquinas by modern existential and social philosophy.

In this phase of the change there is certainly the danger that existing structures will be excessively reinforced. Many people feel the ground slipping beneath their feet if the thought patterns of two and a half thousand years are to be disregarded. They cling therefore to fundamentalist solutions. Yet every one-sided solution is foredoomed to failure. At best it is postponing a true solution.

We have to find our way to a new consciousness which will be able to integrate earlier archaic, mythological and magical forms. We must find our way to a new simplicity. This is particularly true in the area of religion. For many people the conceptual exposition of religious truths no longer suffices. They no longer look to theology for their salvation, but to faith and the experience of God. This is a typical manifestation and is not to be reckoned as a loss. Above all else, religions have to understand and affirm the new in mankind and in its thinking. If they succeed in that, many people will find their way back.

Looking hopefully into the future

Amidst all the changes demanded of us, we must look more at what is coming. It is like looking at the rising sun in the early morning. While we are gazing at the gradually spreading brightness, the dawn begins to display a rich variety of colour until eventually the sun becomes visible.

Our contribution is to look ahead, mindful and alert. The rest happens of itself. Is not that how it is in our own lives? Do not decisive matters often happen without reference to us, without our being asked about them? What does matter with changes is to see in them the work of God, to watch for that and to be open to it. In all the changes in our life the return of the Lord is heralded. He is approaching us from the future.

We must especially keep in view what happens when the present crisis has been overcome. Whatever we have still to suffer until the next stage is complete is worth the trouble. It will be a new and happier human race. People have not yet reached that measure of spiritual being to which they are destined.

In integrating the new consciousness, Christianity has a heavy task. It must grow out of expressing itself in western systematic thinking as it has done heretofore. It is worth pursuing this way. With the emergence of the new consciousness the right solutions will be reached of their own accord. That goes for the eagerly desired unity of Christian confessions, for progress in dialogue with other religions and also for our efforts to bring about peace in the world.

In the process of change, which equally engages both the church and the world, may we see the One who is to come.

The Lord who is coming again

During his earthly life, Jesus often emphasised the advent of the new by reference to the coming of the kingdom of God. In the light of their experience of the resurrection, the disciples recognised that in Jesus himself the kingdom of God had dawned. They expected the Lord to return soon. In the course of time this expectation receded and faith became domesticated. We have to renew this expectation and to rediscover that in the change taking place in our times he is already coming.

We must arouse once more that longing for the Lord to come soon. The deer thirsts for running waters, so shall our souls thirst for the Lord. As a pregnant woman awaits the birth of her child, we shall await his coming.

This is very beautifully expressed in the *Spiritual Exercises of*

Gertrude the Great: 'When, when will you show me yourself, so that I may see you and with joy may have confidence in you, oh God? ... Beloved countenance, when will you satisfy me? ... When will I be favoured with your embrace, when behold you, God of my heart ... Soon, soon let me rejoice in seeing your countenance.'[3] This yearning grows until the soul returns to Christ, when the whole world will become radiant in it.

'The whole creation has been groaning in travail together until now; and not only the creation, but we ourselves, who have the first fruits of the Spirit, groan inwardly as we await the adoption of sons, the redemption of our bodies' (Rom 8:22-23). The experience of incompletion is in a special way a time of prayer. Often we do not know exactly what we should pray for. 'The Spirit himself intercedes for us with sighs too deep for words' (Rom 8:26). Prayer and the sighs of the Spirit alternate in Paul. In prayer we renew our waiting for the Lord.

Fullness of life

We are waiting for the full life. Heretofore life has been growth in bits and pieces. Eventually the seed must become a great tree and the birds of heaven come to dwell in the treetops.

There is much in the life of individuals, the faith community and indeed the whole of humanity which remains fragmented. We are still hanging on to cultural barriers, differences of race and nation. We need someone else to overcome distinctions between 'Jews and Greeks, slaves and freemen, man and woman, in order to discover that we are all one in Christ Jesus' (cf. Gal 3:28).

Instead of advancing to the heart of our faith, we halt at the externals, which are all transitory. The Revelation of John says that in the holy city, the new Jerusalem, there will be no temple, for the Lord is its temple, and the Lamb (cf. Rev 21:23). When all is perfected in God all the different forms of piety will fall away and the relationship of people with God will be characterised by friendship. This inner relationship is worth more than all the systems and structures of religious mediation, all norms and prescriptions, the cult of his glory and the hierarchical structure of the church. When at last we meet the Lord he will outshine all of that.

We shall find our way there to an all embracing community of brothers and sisters. We will be able to build a community, to rule in peace and joy, and above all in love. Differences will no longer be an obstacle; on the contrary, they will be an enrichment.

Our lifetime is a vigil of the *Parousia*.* We are challenged to be ready and able for the return of the Lord. May we have watchful hearts and be at home when he comes, as Mary was when the angel visited her. May he bestow on us a heart ready and able to accept his call when he comes. May we be alert and not sleep through the sunrise of the new and everlasting life. May we await the Lord with a joyous heart, as Mary awaited the birth of her son. May we understand ever more deeply what Christian life means: to be born, to grow to fullness of life. The new life begins as a tiny mustard seed, then grows to be a great tree, in which the birds of heaven come to dwell.

GLOSSARY

Meaning of the following words only as they are used in the text:

Angst: cf. below under *Existential.*

Archetype: a perfect symbol of a spiritual reality.

Christological: from christology, theology concerning Christ.

Doctor of the Church: a title traditionally used to acclaim the excellence of a Catholic writer's teaching; now a title conferred by the Pope on canonised writers, confirming the high value of their teaching.

Ecclesiology: theology concerning the Church.

Eschatological: concerning the last things, the end time, the after life.

Existential angst: acute anxiety or remorse, undefined, but connected with personal experiences.

Fathers of the Church: a title used for the early writers on Christian doctrine.

Fixation: condition of being set in a certain way of doing or thinking; obsession

Genre: kind or category of literary work.

Johannine: referring to the writings of the New Testament ascribed to St John.

Locution: words or expressions that are experienced as spoken and as supernatural in origin.

Mariology: theology concerning Mary.

Marist: relating to five religious groups --- priests, brothers, laity, and two groups of sisters, originating from a project for a Society of Mary (c.1812-1816); also to their works and spirituality.

Metaphysical: from metaphysics, the philosophy of being; commonly used to mean abstract reasoning.

Monotheism: belief or doctrine that there is only one God.

Parousia: The Greek word for what is commonly called the Second Coming of Christ in Judgement, at the end of history.

Pauline: referring to St Paul, his thought and missionary foundations.

Philosophia perennis: a basic understanding, considered to be always and everywhere valid.

Pneumatology: theology concerning the Holy Spirit.

Type: a symbol of a spiritual reality.

Brief reference to some of the people named in this book. We do not include contemporary writers or generally well known figures, saints, etc.

d'Agreda, Maria, early eighteenth century Spanish mystic, author of *The Mystical City of God,* purporting to be a life of Mary.

Angelus Silesius, literary name of Joseph Scheffler, 1624-77. A convert to Catholicism and prolific writer of the Catholic reaction to the Reformation. Produced four volumes of religious poetry, characterised by deep love for Jesus and awareness of the stages of the mystical life.

Ambrose, St, 340-97, Bishop of Milan, writer, (Father of the Church), developer of hymnody; fearless opponent of intrusion by Imperial authorities.

Anselm, St, 1033-1109. Norman, Archbishop of Canterbury, one of the founders of medieval 'scholastic' philosophy, theology.

Augustine, St, 354-430 son of St Monica, converted by the preaching of Ambrose (q.v.) Doctor of the Church, Bishop of Hippo in North Africa. Founded a monastic community, most notable for his teaching on grace, for his voluminous writings and their enormous influence on the western church.

Aristotle, 384-22 BC. Athenian, student of Plato (cf below) but based his thinking on observation of phenomena and examination of thinking process and language. Author of many original treatises on logic, natural history, physics. Through Thomas Aquinas (q.v), and medieval philosophy, influential to our day.

Bernard, St, 1090-1153, monk of Citeaux, founder of Clairveaux Abbey, mystic, adversary of Abelard's rationalism, promoted devotion to 'Our Lady'. Widely influential in the contemporary world.

Bede,Venerable, 673-735, Anglo-Saxon monk, spiritual writer and historian.

Bonaventure, St, 1221-1274, Italian Franciscan, Doctor of the Church, General of the order. Combined preaching, teaching, writing, administration with contemplative prayer.

Borchert, Wolfgang, 1921-47, dramatist, one of the first to express reactions to the war and its aftermath.

Boudon, Henri-Marie, 1624-1702, archdeacon of Evreux, reformer of the clergy, survived ten years of scandalous misrepresentation and wrote while on missions. Best known for *The Love of Jesus in the Blessed Sacrament* and *God Alone,* both influential among the early Marists.

Brecht, Berthold, 1898-1956, writer and left-wing pacifist, controversialist. In exile 1933-47, then returned to East Berlin. Best known as dramatist.

Brigid, St, 1303-73, Swedish ruler, famous for her *Revelations.*

Chaminade, Guillaume, French priest, founder of the Marianists, also called 'Society of Mary' contemporary of the Marist founders, but with different approach to marian spirituality.

Cloriviere, Pierre-Joseph, 1735-1820, French Jesuit, spiritual writer.

Daries, Bernard, French cleric who, in the 1790s together with Fr Cloriviere proposed but did not establish a 'Society of Mary'. Their proposal was unknown to the Marist Fathers.

Delp, Alfred, 1907-45, German Jesuit, convert, theologian, sociologist, active in Catholic social publicity and organisation, until stopped by the Nazi government. Executed. Letters, reports, meditations, published after his death.

Colin, Jean Claude, 1790-1875, founder of the Society of Mary, Marist Fathers, and co-founder of the Marist Sisters. Also part of the project, the Marist Brothers, founded by a Marist priest, St Marcellin Champagnat, lay branches of the Society, and the Missionary Sisters of the Society of Mary.

Eckart, Meister, 1260-1328, Dominican, Master of the University of Paris, active in the Rhineland, originator of the Rhenish mystical school. Preached widely in the vernacular, demonstrating from scripture the incarnation of God in the human soul. His subtle thought led to some of his ideas and language being misunderstood and condemned.

Eymard, St Peter Julian, 1811-1868, French priest, began ministry as a Marist, then founded the Fathers and Sisters of the Blessed Sacrament to promote eucharistic devotion.

Flüe, St Nicolas von der, 1417-87, national hero and patron saint of Switzerland. Soldier, official, politician, hermit and contemplative.

de Foucauld, Charles, 1858-1916, French priest, hermit and missionary in the Sahara. His spirituality, drawn from contemplation of Nazareth, inspired the lay institute of Little Brothers and Sisters.

Gebser, Jean, 1905-73. Lecturer in psychology (Zurich) and professor of contemporary culture (Salzburg). Noted for developmental theory: sees the present period as integrating previous stages of consciousness and culture. Has influenced New Age movement.

Gertrude, St, 'the Great'. 1256?-1302, Benedictine at Helfta; with Mechthild (qv) one of the great German mystics of the fourteenth century. Practised what was called 'bridal spirituality', in deep personal union with Jesus in the Trinity, but also intense liturgical life; noted *Revelations.*

Gregory Nazianzen, 330-396, *Gregory of Nyssa,* 335-395, associated Greek Doctors of the Church.

Grignion de Montfort, St, missionary in the west of France over the period 1673-1716. Founded the Company of Mary, called Montfortin Fathers, and religious sisters, Daughters of Wisdom.

Grou, Jean Nicolas, 1731-1803, French Jesuit, humanist, controversialist, spiritual director and mystic.

Guardini, Romano, 1885-1968. German theologian, universities of Berlin, Tübingen,Munich. Covered basic questions of religious belief in contemporary literary and cultural context. Foremost in the liturgical and youth movements.

Ignatius of Loyola, St. 1491-1556, Spanish. A gentleman soldier; after deep conversion to Christ and ordination, he and seven companions placed themselves at the service of the Pope for mission. The Jesuits established, 1540. He left a systematic guide to meditation and conversion, *The Spiritual Exercises.*

John of the Cross, St. 1542-91. Spanish Carmelite, religious reformer (with Teresa of Avila, q.v.), mystical poet and theologian. Doctor of the Church, noted for *The Ascent of Mount Carmel, The Dark Night, The Spiritual Canticle.*

Kant, Immanuel, 1724-1804. German philosopher. Held that we cannot know things in themselves, but only through our sense of time and space, nor values in themselves, but only through our moral sense. (e.g. liberty, immortality, existence of God).

Kierkegaard, Søren, 1813-1855, Danish thinker and writer, considerably influenced twentieth-century philosophers of personal existence.

Kübler-Ross, Elizabeth, (*1926), Swiss physician and psychiatrist. Became famous through her book, *On Death and Dying,* where she describes the five stages of dying. Gave countless conferences on this theme.

Lassalle, Hugo Enomiya, German Jesuit, b. 1898, life long ministry in Japan, whence the additional Japanese name 'Enomiya'. Professor at German language University in Tokyo (Sophia), and deeply involved in social work. Wounded by Hiroshima atomic bomb, worked for setting up Peace Church memorial, and thereafter for harmony between Zen and Christianity.

Lessing, Gotthold Ephraim, 1729-81, German literary critic, philosophic dramatist.

Mechthild of Magdeburg, 1210-1297, originally a béguine (form of lay religious life in secular society, widespread in Netherlands and Germany during the Middle Ages). Joined the Benedictines at Helfta. Author of the influential mystical work *The Flowing Light of the Godhead.* cf. Gertrude.

Melanchton, Philip, 1497-1560, leading disciple of Luther, author of the *Confession of Augsburg,* a basic statement of Lutheran belief.

Nietzsche, Friedrich, 1844-1900. German thinker; undertook a brilliantly written critique of western values … esthetic, philosophic, scientific, religious. Some of his ideas highly influential: e.g. the will to power, superman, 'death of God'.

Origen, 185-254, a much referred-to thinker of the early church.

Pascal, Blaise, 1623-62, mathematician, physicist, philosopher, spiritual writer and creative in all these domains. Connected with austere religious community of Port Royal. Notes for an unfinished defence of Christianity collected in the famous *Pensées.*

Plato, 428-348/7 BC, philosopher. Held that truth does not lie in single objects but in 'Ideas', pure types of each group of objects, with the idea of the good at the top. Through St Augustine he has greatly influenced western thinking.

Rahner Karl, 1904-84, German Jesuit, professor of Christianity and religious philosophy, theological writer on contemporary problems, editor of major theological dictionaries, official theologian at Vatican II. Very influential in post Vatican II period.

Stein, Edith, (St Teresa Benedict), 1891-1942, German Jewish convert from atheism, writer on Husserl's philosophy, educational method, feminist theology and spirituality. Entered Carmel, 1932; removed to Auschwitz 1942, and sent to the gas chamber immediately on arrival.

Tauler, Johann, 1300-61, Dominican, disciple of Eckhart, whose teaching he continued through his preaching.

Teilhard de Chardin, Pierre, 1881-1955 French Jesuit, paleontologist, philosopher. Author of a synthesis concluding to the evolution of the universe, ending in a unity and fusion with God.

Teresa of Avila, St. 1515-82. Spanish Carmelite, reformer of the Order (with John of the Cross, q.v.). Doctor of the Church. Mystical writings, notably *The Interior Castle,* a synthesis of her teaching on prayer as a way to encounter with Christ.

Thomas Aquinas St, 1225-74, Doctor of the Church, Italian Dominican, taught in Paris. His teaching makes use of Aristotle's philosophical framework, and centres around the theme of harmony between faith and reason. His *Summa Theologica,* always highly regarded, functioned as an authoritative manual of Catholic theology from the 1880s to Vatican II.

NOTES

CHAPTER I

1. Karl Rahner, *Schriften zur Theologie Bd XIV*, Einsiedeln 60, 370, in English: Theological Investigations, vol 20, translated by Edward Quinn, London 81, 149fwd.
2. Carlo Carretto, *Beata te che hai creduto, Roma 80*. In English: *Blessed are you who believed*, Tumbrigde Wells 82,11-13.
3. Ignatius of Loyola, *Spiritual Exercises*, translated and edited by L.J. Puhl, Chicago 50, 52f (Nr. 110-117).
4. For Matthew Jesus is the new Moses, whose coming is from the beginning endangered but he will be saved by God's miraculous intervention.
5. Jesus himself had this view of the hidden greatness of people. He realises a poor woman putting a few coppers in the Temple treasury has given more than many rich people. He sees the humility of the tax-gatherer was worth more than the gestures of the Pharisee, and perceives the basic goodness of the prodigal son and the good thief on the cross. John teaches us to develop awareness for what is hidden, encourages us to discover the hidden treasure of the Kingdom of God, and not to overlook the precious pearl.
6. cf. Jean Coste, Nazareth in the thought of Father Colin, ACTA S.M.,Nr. 31 (Sept 61), 301 fwd.
7. Ignatius of Loyola, *Spiritual Exercises*, ibid. 119 (Nr. 271)
8. Mary is only mentioned twice in John's gospel, but in decisive circumstances: at the beginning of Jesus' ministry (Cana), and the end (Calvary).
9. cf. Perspectives of Vat II, in *Lumen Gentium* chapter 8.
10. Ignatius of Loyola, *Spiritual Exercises*, ibid, 95 fwd. (Nr.218-225).
11. Jean Coste, *The Role of Mary at the birth of the Church and the end of time*. ACTA S.M. Nr. 27 (Dec 59), 419-428
12. 'The Blessed Virgin said: "I was the support of the new-born Church; I shall be also at the end of time. My embrace will be open to all who wish to come to me."' *A Founder Speaks*, translated by Antony Ward, Rome 75, 40 (doc.4§1). This is a reference, often repeated, to the founding impetus of the Society of Mary at Le Puy, where in 1812 Jean Courveille felt himself addressed by Mary.
13. Constitutions of the Society of Mary of 1872, Rome 92, nos. 49-50.
14. 'Among congregations claiming to be Marian that of the Marist Fathers is one of the least marian and one of the most marian' Jean Coste, the place of Mary among the Marists Today (SM Doc 1), Rome 73,12. And as explanation it was added: 'The least marian in the sense that it promotes no particular marian devotions, does not look to Mary as a model placed in front of it to be imitated; and yet the most marian, in that it attempts an identification with Mary's own consciousness, with Mary's own viewpoint in looking out on

to the world and the church and their needs' Michael Fitzgerald, A Marian consciesness (Maristica 5), Rome 91, 58 .

CHAPTER II

1. Edith Stein, *Ewiges und Endliches Sein*, Freiburg 86, 21f, in English: *Finite and Eternal Being*, see: Edith Stein, *Selected Writings*, translated and edited by S. M. Bathdorff, Springfield 90.

2. Edith Stein, *Kreuzeswissenschaft*, Freiburg 83, 265, in English: *The Science of the Cross – A study on John of the Cross*, edited by D. Gelber, Chicago 60.

3 Bernard v Clairvaux, in: *Gotteserfahrung und Wege in die Welt*, hrsg. B. Schellenberger, Freiburg 82, 74.

4. Edith Stein, *Ewiges und Endliches Sein*, Freiburg 86,a.a.O. 405, in English: Finite and Eternal Being, ibid.

5. André Louf, Signeur apprends- nous a prier, Bruxelles 73 , in English: *Teach us to pray*, Boston 92,31.

6. Vgl. Emmanuel Jungclaussen, *Das Jesusgebet*, Regensburg 94, In English: *On the invocation of the name of Jesus*, London 70; Cp. The way of a pilgrim, translated by R. French, London 95.

7. Edith Stein, *Ewiges und Endliches Sein*, Freiburg 86, 13, in English: *Finite and Eternal Being*,ibid.

8. Brixner, *Die Mystiker*, Augsburg 87, 17

9. Ignatius of Loyola , *Spiritual Exercises*, ibid. 101f, (Nr.234)

10. J. Coste, *Nazareth*, ibid. 304

11. Teresa of Avila, *The Interior Castle* in: *The complete works of Saint Teresa of Jesus*, translated and edited by Allison Peers, Vol II, London 46, 259f.

12. Therèse of Lisiuex, *Histoire d `une Ame*, Paris 53, in English: *The Story of a Soul*, translated by Michael Day, London 64.

13. Jean Coste, *Lectures on Society of Mary History*, Rome 65, 164

14. Jean-Claude Colin, *A Founder Speaks*, Rome 75, 350 (doc. 120,§1).

15. Edith Stein, *Welt und Person – Beiträge zum christlichen Wahrheitsstreben*, Freiburg 62, 159. Cp. in English: *Knowledge – truth-being*, see: Edith Stein, *Selected Writings*, Translated and edited by S. M. Bathdorff, Springfield 90.

16. John of the Cross, *The Dark Night*, in: John of the Cross, The collected works, translated by Kieran Kavanough, Washington 73, 350-352.

17. Fernando Urbina, Dunkle Nacht-Weg in die Freiheit Johannes vom Kreuz und sein Denken, Salzburg 86, 31.f

18. John of the Cross, The Ascent of Mount Carmel, in: John of the Cross, The collected works, ibid. 126

19. John of the Cross, *The Dark Night*, in: John of the Cross, The collected works, ibid. 351.

20. Sandra Schneiders, *Contemporary religious life – death or transformation*, New York 97, 27-29.

21. Elisabeth Kübler- Ross, *On Death and Dying*, Indianapolis 91.

22. Dennis and Matthew Linn, *Healing Life's Hurts*, New York 78.
23 Constititutions of the Society of Mary of 1872, Rome 92, Nr. 50.
24. Jean Claude Colin, *A Founder speaks*, ibid. 379 (Nr.132. § 28).

CHAPTER III

1. Karl Rahner, *Schriften zur Theologie*, Bd XIV, a.a.O. 370, in English: *Theological Investigations*, vol. 20, ibid, 149f.
2. Geoffrey Robinson, Signposts for an emerging church. In: The Mix (96/1), ed. Michael Whelan.
3. Pascal, *Pensées*, edited in French and English by. H. F. Stewart, London 50.
4. Paul VI, 'Evangelii nuntiandi', no. 14, 18, 41, 19
5 John Paul II, Redemptoris missio. Nos. 67, 37.
6. For more extensive treatment see for example: O. Chadwick,. *History of Christianity*, 1995; P. Johnson, History of Christianity, 1972; P. Hughes, *Popular History of the Catholic Church*. 1952.
7. Walbert Bühlmann, *Wo der Glaube lebt – Einblicke in die Lage der Weltkirche*, Freiburg 78, in English: The coming of the third church – An analysis of the present and future of the church, Am Arber 80.
8. For further reading, for example: A. Richardson & J. Bowden, eds. *New Dictionary of Christian Theology* (SMC 1983); H. Glazrea & M. Hellwig eds, *Modern Catholic Encyclopedia* (Gill & Macmillan) 1994; F. Cross & E. Livingstone, eds, *Oxford Dictionary of the Christian Church* (Oxford University Press 1997) *Encyclopedia of Theology*, ed. Karl Rahner (Burns & Oates) 1975; *A New Dictionary of Theology*, ed. Michael Glazier & others, Delaware, 1987.
9. Max Thurian, *Mary, Mother of the Lord, Figure of the Church*, London 1963, 50
10. Cf. Gerald Arbuckle, *Out of Chaos, refounding religious congregations*, New York, 88.
11. For the adaption of the processes of dying to social changes, cf. Gerald Arbuckle, *Grieving for change – a spirituality for refounding gospel communities*, London, 91.
12. Enomiya Lassalle, *Wohin geht der Mensch?*, Freiburg 88, 19-31.

TOWARDS A NEW HUMANITY DIGRESSION

1. For further reading, cf. Pierre Teilhard de Chardin, *Le phenomene humain*, in English, *The Phenomenon of Man*, New York, 59; Jean Gebser, *Ursprung und Gegenwart*, München, 68; Enomiya Lassalle, *Wohin geht der Mensch?*, Freiburg, 88 .
2. Immanuel Kant, *Was ist Aufklärung*, Göttingen, 67, 55 in English: *What is enlightment?* Chicago, 49.
3. Gertrud die Große, *Exercitia Spiritualia*, in: Brixner, *Die Mystiker*, a.a.O. 228